Working for a Family Business

A FAMILY——
BUSINESS
——PUBLICATION

Family Business Publications are the combined efforts of the Family Business Consulting Group and Palgrave Macmillan. These books provide useful information on a broad range of topics that concern the family business enterprise, including succession planning, communication, strategy and growth, family leadership, and more. The books are written by experts with combined experiences of over a century in the field of family enterprise and who have consulted with thousands of enterprising families the world over, giving the reader practical, effective, and time-tested insights to everyone involved in a family business.

FBG, founded in 1994, is the leading business consultancy exclusively devoted to helping family enterprises prosper across generations.

FAMILY BUSINESS LEADERSHIP SERIES

This series of books comprises concise guides and thoughtful compendiums to the most pressing issues that anyone involved in a family firm may face. Each volume covers a different topic area and provides the answers to some of the most common and challenging questions.

Titles include:

All of the books were written by members of the Family Business Consulting Group and are based on both our experiences with thousands of client families as well as our empirical research at leading research universities the world over.

Working for a Family Business

A Non-Family Employee's Guide to Success

Christopher J. Eckrich
and Stephen L. McClure

palgrave
macmillan

First published by the Family Business Consulting Group Publications, 2004.

This edition first published in 2011 by
PALGRAVE MACMILLAN®
in the United States—a division of St. Martin's Press LLC,
175 Fifth Avenue, New York, NY 10010.

Where this book is distributed in the UK, Europe and the rest of the
world, this is by Palgrave Macmillan, a division of Macmillan Publishers
Limited, registered in England, company number 785998, of Houndmills,
Basingstoke, Hampshire RG21 6XS.

Palgrave Macmillan is the global academic imprint of the above companies
and has companies and representatives throughout the world.

Palgrave® and Macmillan® are registered trademarks in the United States,
the United Kingdom, Europe and other countries.

ISBN: 978-0-230-11114-1

Library of Congress Cataloging-in-Publication Data

Eckrich, Christopher J.
    Working for a family business : a non-family employee's guide to
success / by Christopher J. Eckrich and Stephen L. McClure.
        p. cm. — (Family business leadership series)
    Originally published: Marietta, Ga. : Family Enterprise Pub., c2004.
    Includes bibliographical references and index.
    ISBN 978–0–230–11114–1
        1. Family-owned business enterprises. 2. Employee handbooks. I.
McClure, Stephen L. II. Title.

HD62.25.E27 2011
650.1—dc22   2010036207

A catalogue record of the book is available from the British Library.

Design by Newgen Imaging Systems (P) Ltd., Chennai, India.

First Palgrave Macmillan edition: January 2011

10 9 8 7 6 5 4 3 2 1

Printed in the United States of America.

Contents

Exhibits

Chapter 1

Introduction

Your Role in a Special Partnership

In a newspaper interview not long ago, Richard Yuengling Jr., the fifth-generation owner of D. G. Yuengling & Son Brewery in Pottsville, Pennsylvania, credited the company's non-family executive vice president, David Casinelli, with the company's recent rapid growth. Said Yuengling: "He's put us where we are today."[1]

As the Yuengling case points out, non-family employees are often the key to family business success. Yet, one of the most challenging and confusing roles in a family firm is that of non-family supervisor or executive. And one of the least understood relationships is that between family members and key non-family employees. Consider these all-too-typical scenarios:

> **Scenario #1.** The family managers and shareholders of Peerless Electronics are thrilled when Alan Woods, long a star senior executive in a much larger, public company, agrees to become Peerless's chief operating officer. After a few months, however, this new non-family executive lets his exasperation show. "There's too much family in this place!" he declares. Secretly, some of the other non-family employees agree. They don't understand why the CEO's daughter was given an important job when she can only work part-time, or why his brother is always putting his two cents in, or why the CEO puts up with

those ungrateful minority shareholders, who also happen to be his nieces and nephews. Besides, many family members voice strong opinions, sometimes opposing each other on important issues.

In Alan's opinion, the business would function much better if the family got out of the way. "Then we could run this place like a business," he mutters.

Scenario #2. Olivia Turner wonders if she should start hunting for a new job. She has been working at Northam Tools for six years, and a year ago, was named head of her department. But the founder is ailing and, ever since his wife died last year, the grown-up children, who all work at Northam, have been bickering openly. Olivia doubts the company can continue to be successful once it falls into the hands of the siblings. All they do is fight. And it's too bad. Olivia really loves her job, but with so much tension swirling around and so much fear about the company's future, she thinks she may have to move on. If she does, it'll be a major loss for Northam because she is very talented and hardworking.

Scenario #3. Justin, a relatively new non-family CFO at Miller Transport, gets an earful one day from Adam Miller, 36, the son of the founder/CEO of the family-owned company. "Dad is really behind the times," complains Adam, the company's executive vice president. "This business is going downhill and it will fail unless we update our technology and adopt some new strategies. It's really time I took over leadership, but I just can't get the old man to listen to me."

Justin has seen the need for succession for a while, agrees with Adam, and at the next opportunity, he confronts Adam's father. "You know, Bob, you might want to be stepping up your retirement plans," Justin says. "Adam's really ready to pick up the reins, and besides, I think he's right about the need for change."

"What do you know about it?" Bob snarls. "Adam's not anywhere near ready, and, as I have told him, he's got some pretty crazy ideas about how to run this place." It was clear that the conversation was over. Justin is stunned. He was just trying to be helpful, and, after all, Bob had been talking about retirement ever since Justin arrived at the company.

These stories suggest how confusion and misunderstanding can drag a company down and derail or at least sidetrack careers. In the last scenario, Justin miscalculates his position with Bob and endangers his employment. While the son may be right, Justin has taken sides and alienated the father, his boss. In the second scenario, Olivia, an excellent performer, doesn't really understand what she's seeing: typical behavior on the part of adult siblings undergoing crisis. And, because she doesn't understand, she's getting ready to jump ship, which will deprive the company of a valued non-family employee. In the first scenario, Alan Woods demonstrates a complete lack of knowledge of what family businesses are like. He comes from the corporate world and becomes overwhelmed because he has no experience with family firms. Because of his background, he doesn't understand how to work toward a happy middle ground.

To be sure, business-owning families often don't understand themselves very well and often don't know what it takes to get the best out of their non-family employees. They will find this book helpful, but even more helpful if they share it with some "significant" others—key non-family employees, board members, advisors, shareholders, and other family members, including in-laws.

Working for a Family Business is designed first and foremost for key non-family employees. If you are a non-family employee who shoulders substantial responsibility or holds a position of considerable influence, this book is especially for you. Perhaps you are a department head who runs manufacturing, marketing, sales, finance, purchasing, information technology, or some other major function. Perhaps you hold an important supervisory or administrative role, overseeing public relations or engineering. Or perhaps you are an office manager, or the executive assistant to a senior manager. We've written this book with you in mind. The size or type of business you're in doesn't matter. The principles for success as a non-family employee apply to virtually all industries.

This book is also for you if you sit on the board of directors of a family business or serve it as an advisor—accountant, attorney, banker, or insurance agent. Much of what applies to a key employee will also apply to you in serving the family business.

This book will benefit you in many ways. First, it will provide you with a greater understanding of the concept of "family business." Family businesses are unlike other companies, and you will learn how they differ and how those differences impact you and what you do.

Out of this understanding, you will gain insight into the family and its behavior, as well as develop greater empathy for the family as it attempts to meet its own difficult, predictable challenges. You will come to recognize normal behavior patterns in business families and, as a result, you should feel more comfortable and less worried about what you see. You will be more able to grapple with issues and questions such as: Is this business in trouble? Is it going to be sold? What if I have to supervise the boss's daughter, or mentor a nephew? What does all this family disagreement mean?

You will discover some no-win traps to avoid, find tools and techniques for handling difficult situations, and develop judgment about your ability to take on certain roles or intervene in sensitive family situations. Generally, this book should provide you with the family business knowledge you need to be successful in your job and your career.

Finally, we will show you how best to serve the family and the business to insure the success of both. You will come to recognize the importance of seeing yourself as the family's partner.

When you can do that, you serve yourself best as well. It is likely that your goal is to be so indispensable to the business that the family appreciates you, makes your job secure, and rewards you well. Absorbing the insights offered here will help you achieve that complex goal.

Chapter 2

What Makes a Family Business Unique?

"Everybody's like family," is how Ernie Houston explained why he still enjoyed working for Melrose Diner, after more than 40 years of employment there. A family-owned Philadelphia restaurant founded in 1935, Melrose Diner was named one of the country's best places to work.[2]

"Our job is to make this a good place to work for our employees, and it's their job to make this a good place to eat for our customers," Richard Kubach Jr., owner and son of the restaurant's founder, told the *Philadelphia Inquirer.*[3] The Kubach family philosophy has made Melrose Diner a local institution, beloved by employees and customers alike. Some regulars eat three meals a day at the Melrose. Now the third-generation, Kubach's daughter and son, are working in the business with their father, carrying on the family's employee- and customer-friendly traditions.

Ernie Houston's affection for the business he works for is not at all rare when it comes to family-owned companies. Time and again, we hear employees of companies say, "They treat me like family here," or, "They really care about me." How often do you hear that same sentiment from people who work in large public corporations?

As a non-family employee, you are already aware of some of the challenges of working for a family business. When multiple cousins become employed, family and work relations can become quite complex. Family members may fight with one another and create tension for everyone else. An owner might hire a family member who makes little or no contribution to the organization, or Aunt Emma, who owns one percent of the company, calls and asks the head of shipping to send someone over to her house to move furniture for her.

But there is a brighter side to family business. Family-owned companies are unique in many positive respects. When you understand that, you might find yourself saying, "Hmmmmm, I'm pretty lucky to be working here. Let me see how I can make the most of this experience."

For starters, here's what non-family employees tell us:

—"Our company has a culture of being concerned and caring for our people. This stems from the owners."

—"What I really like is that we have less paranoia around short-term quarterly reports. Last year, we adopted a new strategy that will not pay off immediately, but will assure the long-term health of the company. This gives me hope as an employee."

—"One thing that makes this family business unique is that when economic times are poor, shareholders are willing to cut their own dividends for the sake of the long-term outlook and the health of the company. I find this very encouraging."

—"There is a culture of giving in our company. One owner heads a foundation that created a park. Employees here are allowed to do some volunteer work on company time."

Family firms often offer more security and more opportunity to make a difference. William M. Reid is the non-family president and CEO of the Mechanics Bank, a family-controlled financial institution based in Richmond, California. Mechanics has about 30 branches, and as Reid told us, "We're a really good company. We've had terrific success over a long period of time and [Mechanics] is a very strong and stable company. It's a wonderful place to work." As CEO of such an enterprise, he notes, "one can have long-term influence and in a way that is different than with a publicly held company."

Family firms have a reputation for paying less than many publicly held counterparts, and Reid admits that that is the case at his company. But, he adds, Mechanics is "an attractive place to work, it is more secure, it is more predictable. The working environment is one that is more pleasant to be around. It's more collaborative. It is supportive of the long-term growth of employees more, I think, than the public companies that I'm familiar with. All those things make it a happier place to be to do one's work."

GOOD FOR THE ECONOMY

Family-owned firms make a significant contribution to the worldwide economy. Statistical research on family firms is still in its infancy, but the International Family Enterprise Research Academy (IFERA) contends that family business is the dominant form of business throughout the world.[4]

In the United States alone, depending on how you define family business, researchers Joseph H. Astrachan and Melissa Carey Shanker suggest that in the year 2000, family firms contributed anywhere from $2.6 trillion (or 29 percent) to $5.9 trillion (or 64 percent) to the U.S. Gross Domestic Product. They estimate that family businesses employ from 36 million people (27 percent of the U.S. workforce) to 82 million (62 percent of the workforce).[5]

Family-owned firms make a significant contribution to the worldwide economy.

While people tend to think of family business as small business, many of the nation's largest companies are family-owned or family-controlled. Think of Ford Motor Company, the New

York Times Company, S. C. Johnson & Son, Marriot Hotels, or Anheuser Busch. Studies indicate that anywhere from 37 percent to 47 percent of the *Fortune* 500 companies can be called family businesses.[6]

Family businesses also show considerable staying power. According to the 2003 American Family Business Survey, a study of 1,143 U.S. family-owned businesses, the companies reported mean annual revenues of $36.5 million, up more than 50 percent from 1997 to 2002. The combined revenue of these companies was $54.4 billion. Despite adverse economic conditions, these firms had not decreased company employment levels in the three years ending in 2002.[7]

Studies indicate that anywhere from 37 percent to 47 percent of the *Fortune* 500 companies can be called family businesses.

As if to echo the survey's finding that **family businesses often retain their commitment to employees in hard times,** Herbert E. Stoller, CEO of Widmer Interiors, a contract supplier of office and healthcare furnishings based in Peoria, Illinois, told us that fiscal 2003 was a very tough year financially. But the Stoller family resisted laying off any of its 40 employees. "That would be the easiest, quickest way to save money, and we just didn't feel that that would be the right thing to do," said Stoller. The family members believe that they are stewards of the business and have pledged themselves to manage it well for others. You'll learn more about the Stollers in later chapters.

FLEXIBILITY IS GREATER

At their best, family firms are less bureaucratic and can therefore be more flexible and creative in the way they do business. Often, the needs and abilities of the family itself drive strategy. We've known situations where a family-owned retail business had seven outlets because there were seven siblings to run them, or where a new division was created to make the use of the particular talents of one family member. They can be more responsive to a local market because they are not bound by the same requirement that national chain stores have to keep things standard throughout the country with only slight modifications for a particular locale.

...family firms are less bureaucratic and can therefore be more flexible and creative in the way they do business.

Companies that expand beyond their country's borders often discover that being family owned is a great asset. Binswanger Companies, a third-generation commercial real estate company, found that foreign clients like dealing with multigenerational family firms because they can talk to the decision maker and decisions can be made quickly. Now run by two cousins, Binswanger has more than 5,000 employees in 160 offices around the world.[8]

WHAT REALLY MAKES FAMILY BUSINESSES UNIQUE

Family involvement is what really sets family firms apart. This is where non-family employees can play a very major role. For while family involvement is what makes family businesses great, it also makes them a more complex management challenge. Let's explore your role by taking a look at one of the classic models used to understand family businesses.

This model identifies a family business as a series of systems, and provides insight into the various roles held by stakeholders. The three circles represent three systems: the ownership system,

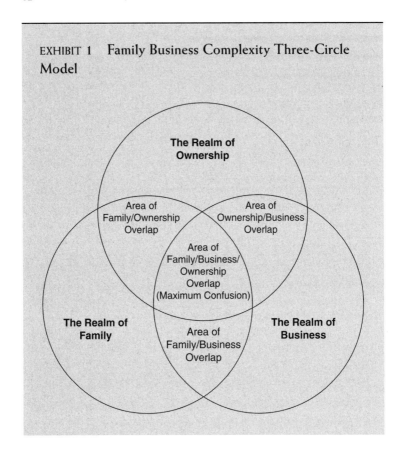

EXHIBIT 1   Family Business Complexity Three-Circle Model

the management system, and the family system. We will refer to these collectively as the family business system.

Notice how the circles overlap. For example, all family members exist somewhere in the family circle. Family members who don't work in the business and have no ownership stake in it are represented in the lower part of the family circle. Though not owners or managers, they may possess a high emotional stake in the business because they have grown up with it and it bears the family name. Other family members may work in the business but own no shares. Still, other family members may own stock but not work in the business. Still others wear all the hats: family member, shareholder, and employee. They are represented by the space in the intersection of the three circles.

Because these roles overlap, family members and employees often have difficulty sorting out which roles a person is playing at any moment in time. For example, a CEO's daughter works in the business. She is often late for work after dropping her children off at childcare. The CEO knows she needs disciplining and may wonder, "Should I confront her as her employer, or have a talk with her as a concerned father?" Her brother, who also works in the business, complains to the CEO about how she is overpaid, though his strong feelings come mostly from his belief that dad always treated her leniently. Meanwhile, a non-family employee wonders whether this is an employee performance issue to be confronted, or a family issue that should remain undiscussed.

It is common in any business to focus mostly on the role of those who work in the business. As the model implies, however, special attention is given to family members who may or may not become employees, but who must prepare themselves to become effective shareholders—a role that, in the case of younger family members, may not occur for years. These family members will someday have a critical role in determining the future direction of the organization.

GOVERNANCE IS DIFFERENT

The way family businesses are governed is also different from governance in non-family companies. Many of the most success-ful business-owning families believe they have almost a "moral imperative" to try to hold the family together. Toward that end, they seek to achieve excellent governance, which is the relation-ship between ownership, management, and the board.

In the beginning, governance is pretty simple. The founder owns the business and has the authority to make all the decisions about how it is to be run. In some cases, it may be a founding partnership that runs the business.

As the business grows or as ownership gets dispersed to members of the second and third generation, governance becomes more complicated. Some families create a board of directors, often consisting of some family members and professional advisors. Other families go further, establishing an independent board, with several key family owners as members plus several highly knowledgeable, qualified outsiders—such as CEOs from other firms. The board represents the shareholders—that is, the owning family—in giving direction to the business and making major decisions (such as whether or not to make an acquisition). In many instances, it also oversees the process of succession.

> Governance is the relationship between ownership, management, and the board.

In larger, more sophisticated, sometimes older businesses, the family develops a parallel system of governance as a means of attending to shared family concerns, such as giving commitment and support to the business or seeing to it that the values of the family are expressed through the enterprise that it owns. As the board of directors governs the business, the family's governing body called a family council, helps guide the family. It is a place for the family to develop a unified voice to provide needed and appropriate input to the board and management. For an in-depth treatment of the topic, see *Family Business Governance: Maximizing Family and Business Potential* by Craig E. Aronoff, Ph.D., and John L. Ward, Ph.D.

Exhibit 2 illustrates how the family governance system and the business governance system work together.

DIFFICULT ISSUES ARE NORMAL

The savviest non-family employees learn to regard the difficult issues of blending family and business as normal and do not

EXHIBIT 2   Family and Business Governance

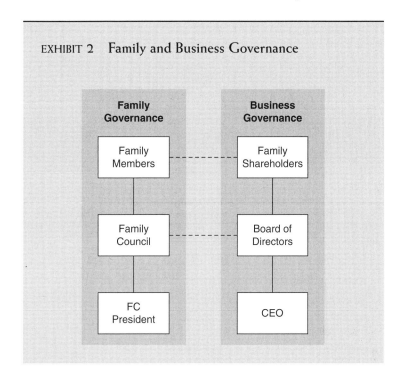

overreact when eruptions occur. They take it upon themselves to understand family business dynamics, beginning with the three-circle model, and to develop an appreciation for the challenge that the family faces in trying to manage a business successfully and preserve it for future generations. They constantly look for ways to help the family separate business, ownership, and family issues—for the good of the family and the business. In doing so, they provide a unique service to a unique enterprise.

Chapter 3

The Value of "Family" to a Family Business

A re there days when you think the business you work for would be a whole lot better off if those noisy and combative family members weren't involved? Then you could just get on with your job—being chief financial officer, second shift supervisor, head of sales, graphic arts designer, chief engineer, director of marketing, or customer service representative. It's natural to feel that way at times. Board members and professional advisors often feel that way, too. The family, with all its problems, sometimes gets in the way of running the business like a business.

But the family is not the enemy. In fact, the business needs the family and is better off for their involvement. It's important to look at the entire situation and to work *with* the family, not against it.

THE FAMILY'S IMPRINT ON THE FIRM

One of the most important things that families do is to establish the set of values that guide how the business will be run. Good, solid values enhance business success, and family culture can influence a company in many positive ways.

Consider Maple Leaf Farms, based in Milford, Indiana. Founded in 1958, owned and run by the Tucker family, the company is acknowledged as the largest producer of duck products in North America.

The three members of the third generation, brothers Scott and John Tucker, who are co-presidents of the company, and their sister, Tricia Rice, a member of the Tucker Family Council—have been holding "successor team" meetings to prepare themselves for their roles as future owners. Not long ago they met to articulate the family's values. They were getting nowhere until Scott asked the question, "Why are we doing this?"

The answer quickly became obvious: "Identifying values is important so that we can be clear among ourselves what our values are, so that we can remain consistent with them in our company, and so that we can properly orient new family members (that is, spouses) as well as maturing ones. Doing so also **helps us clearly explain our values to non-family employees, board members, and advisors who need to know why we do certain things and why we would never consider doing other things, even though they might be common practices in the industry or with our competitors.**"

The siblings identified the Tucker family values as "The Six Fs"—family, food, friends, fun, financial security, and fulfillment. With great excitement, they began to discuss what the company had done in the previous ten years because of those values. Here are some of their results:

- **Family.** Our employees include members of the same family—sometimes from several generations. We offer scholarship programs that assist families in the development of their members.

- **Food.** We hold internal food tastings for new products before they go to market. Nationally, we educate chefs and students on the preparation of duck in order to promote quality at the customer level.

- **Friends.** We encourage friendships among our employees and with our customers. We have a tradition of family events, such as baby showers, family picnics and amusement park visits. Even when people leave Maple Leaf Farms, we try to retain them as friends—we don't let the "doors hit departing employees on their way out."

♦ **Fun.** A visiting chef recently said, "I have gone through lots of processing plants, and I have never seen that many smiling employees working on the lines." We keep things fun with such events as our office Christmas party (held at the company's restaurant), a salsa contest, a chili cook-off and much more.

♦ **Financial security.** We don't sacrifice profit for growth. We make investments for the long-term viability of the company, such as our enhancing investments in animal welfare and bio-security standards, and we balance immediate and long-term needs.

♦ **Fulfillment.** We have a School of Professional Development for employees and participation in it is very good. We foster intellectual development with our educational assistance programs. We also offer bilingual training.

The Tucker siblings presented the values to the family council, which, in turn, decided to engage the management team in the same exercise by asking them the same question: "What are examples of us living our values, and how do we take the next step in thoroughly integrating our values into what we do day in and day out?"

While the Tuckers presented an exceptional example, going through such exercises helps prevent values from getting lost as the younger generation succeeds the parent generation in running and owning a business. Generally, **values are more permanent in a family-owned company and, because they are, non-family employees experience a greater degree of certainty than they might elsewhere.** When a new CEO is brought into a public company, the values of loyalty and longevity may go out the door as the new leader fires existing senior managers and brings in a new team.

Family companies generally have much more stability with respect to what is appropriate and what is not. For the non-family employee, it is just a matter of understanding what the rules are. In general, you'll find that the family cannot tolerate the business operating in a way that is inconsistent with the family's identity and the values that make up that identity. If you're working for a family that takes pride in doing things "the right way," or that says, "Integrity above all else," you know there will be no corners cut in the manufacture of products and no making promises that can't be kept. In fact, many family firms resist change, in part because of the skepticism they direct toward innovations that might conflict with their values.

Another way the family makes its mark on a business is by defining the corporate culture. And corporate culture, of course, reflects values. Entrepreneurial families foster entrepreneurial behaviors among their non-family employees throughout a company. A perfectionist family nurtures perfection throughout the organization. Hardworking families promote an ethic of hard work. Families with a penchant for community service or a strong belief in philanthropy seek ways as an organization to be involved in their community. They may also seek to engage in philanthropy, not only as individual shareholders, but as a corporate entity.

WHAT CARING OWNERS DO

In many of the most successful family-owned businesses, the family name and identity become inseparable from the business. When you think of the family name, you automatically think of the product or service identified with it. Give it a try. Name the product or service that comes to mind when you think of the following families:

1. Porsche
2. Tyson

3. Michelin
4. Marriott
5. De Beers
6. Mars
7. Levi Strauss
8. Benetton
9. Smucker
10. Heineken

Of course you came up with automobiles, chicken, tires, hotels, diamonds, chocolate candy, jeans, fashion, jams and jellies, and beer—in that order.

In many cases, even though the family name is not on the door, the company is so well known nationally, regionally, or locally that the family behind it is still identified with it. The Johnson family is the power behind Fidelity Investments in Boston. In Italy, the Agnelli family is associated with Fiat Group. In Florida, the Moran family is the automobile dealerships of JM Family Enterprises.

Customers often see the presence of family as a plus. Several years ago, S. C. Johnson & Son, Inc., the Racine, Wisconsin, maker of such household products as Glade®, Pledge®, and Windex®, launched an advertising campaign that emphasized its family connection. In a series of television commercials, the late Samuel C. Johnson, the chairman emeritus, spoke about the core values responsible for his company's five generations of success.

"Our research found that family ownership was a tremendous asset," according to Mark Pacchini, Worldwide Account Director of Foote, Cone & Belding, the advertising agency responsible for the campaign. "For most people, family ownership means that there is a family they can trust standing behind the products."

According to Sam Johnson, "A great family business, no matter its size, has to be more than a financial investment. To survive long term it has to be a social positive for the employees, a benefit for the community, a passion for future generations of the family, and committed to earning the goodwill of the consumer everyday."[9]

In the best of circumstances, the family and its business are not only inseparable, but caring family owners also personally identify with the business' products, customers, and employees. One way they do this is to regard themselves as stewards of capital. The Stoller family, behind Widmer Interiors, has assembled a series of documents and policies that the family members, including in-laws, call "The Widmer Stewardship." In one section, they state, in part:

> We believe we are stewards. A steward is one who manages another's property. What we are working with, then, is not our own, but we are responsible and accountable for doing well with the assets that are placed in our trust. The Owner has provided us the talent, skill and judgment to protect His assets and cause them to become more valuable. Stewardship encourages adding value, but depersonalizes wealth and earnings; stewards see wealth as an economic resource to be applied to creating additional wealth for the Owner and other constituents, and view the risks necessary to strengthen a business as natural and less threatening. The long view makes sense.

CEO Herb Stoller puts it more bluntly: "We can't go just blow this money. It's not ours." The Stollers serve as another example of how a family's values and culture—in this case, strong religious belief—influence a business. Still, the Stollers are sensitive to how their employees might feel. Of their faith, Herb Stoller says, "We try not to wear that on our sleeve too much, because at times that can be troubling to people. But we try to live it."

In our experience, business-owning families who view themselves as stewards do not hoard capital or view the business as their piggybank. Their goals may include investing capital, using it wisely (funding a 401(k) plan or establishing an in-house daycare for employee's children), or doing something with it that makes the world a better place. They look at capital and say, "This is the security of the company. If the company is our baby, then this is the baby's college fund. It goes with the baby. It doesn't belong to the ones who made the deposits."

Another way that family firms demonstrate caring is that they break with policy to provide for the special needs of employees or customers. We've seen it happen time and time again. A company may provide extended health-care coverage for a manager's spouse, who contracted a disease that costs well beyond the scope of the benefit package. When a key non-family employee's mother has a heart attack, the employer allows him to use the corporate plane, even though it's against policy, to go be with his dying mother. Or an apartment-owning family lets a customer with a serious long-term health problem live in her apartment several years rent-free.

Let's go back to Melrose Diner in Philadelphia for a moment. One of the reasons it was recognized as one of the best places to work in the United States, is that it offers a pension plan, benefits, and paid vacations—all unusual in the restaurant business. When the head baker developed an allergy to flour, the Kubach family had the bakery redesigned so that he could continue working. Ernie Houston, the long-term employee mentioned earlier, recalls that decades ago, Richard Kubach Sr., the founder, lent him $500 to help him buy his first house.

EXHIBIT 3   Six Ways a Family Can Benefit a Business

1. The family establishes the values by which the business is to be run, defining what is appropriate and what is not.
2. Its mores influence the culture of the business in positive ways.
3. The family's good name and business become inseparable.
4. The family becomes stewards of the business, preserving it for future generations, using its assets to help others.
5. Family owners bend the rules to provide for special needs of employees or customers.
6. The family focuses on the long-term good of the business, not short-term results.

"When somebody has a crisis, a roadblock in their life, we see if there's something we can do to work with them," Richard Kubach Jr. said.[10]

TAKING THE LONG-TERM VIEW

Most business-owning families hope that their businesses will stay in the family. According to the 2003 American Family Business Survey, 88 percent of the respondents expected the family to continue to control the business in five years. Of those who had identified a successor to the CEO, 85 percent said the successor would be a family member.[11]

A family's desire to have business ownership continue into future generations of the family supports a longer-term view when compared to other companies. That view, in turn, strengthens a family firm's stability. Families with such desires may buck the trends. When in hard times other companies are shutting down research and development, such families may keep R&D going—not just because they're looking at long-term return on investment but because they believe the business needs another niche for the next generation to be secure. They're thinking about taking care of their children. When public companies, under pressure from shareholders, are scratching to realize a larger profit every quarter, business-owning families can be patient, satisfied to earn a payoff at a later date. When an offer to buy the business comes in from a competitor, the family may decide not to sell because they believe one or more of next-generation will want to run it. While it may make great economic sense to sell, that's not the point. They see the business as "something we're *doing* here," not "something we're *owning*" To them, the idea of selling may just reflect someone's short-term focus and seem selfish.

When a family is focused on the long term that means a more secure business. And that means a better situation for non-family employees and their careers.

When public companies, under pressure from shareholders, are scratching to realize a larger profit every quarter, business-owning families can be patient, satisfied to earn a payoff at a later date.

YES, THEY'LL BE INCONSISTENT

What if the family you work for falls short of what we've presented here? The truth is even the best families do from time to time. What we've described are families at their best.

You may find, for example, that "breaking with policy" in your family firm means that the owners keep Marge, the non-family executive assistant, on board long after the mandatory retirement age. Why, you may wonder, doesn't the family enforce its retirement policy? Marge has been at the company forever and her competency slipped long ago. People now work "around" her, bypassing her and finding ways to compensate for what she can no longer do. But Marge is a widow and her children have all left the area. And the fact is the founding CEO for whom she works feels intense loyalty toward her and won't let her go.

While the next generation keeps Marge on board out of respect to their father, they prize accountability, and a recent hire that does not perform according to expectations is dismissed. Seems inconsistent, doesn't it? You might think the family looks weak because it's not dealing with Marge. Depending on the size of the business, it can probably accommodate one or two valued long-term employees and can feel it is being loyal and benevolent.

Or consider two kinds of CEO spouses. In one business, the CEO's wife, who does not work in the business, is a protective mother with strong ideas about how her children should be recognized in the business. Her husband may not know how to handle this desire of hers. From time to time, she shows up at the office with one of her teenage sons. He starts bossing non-family employees around, and people feel helpless and don't know how to respond. They know that if they take on the son, they're taking on the wife, and ultimately, the CEO.

In another business, the wife sees herself as an integral component, instilling the values of the family into the business. On occasion she also brings her children to the office because she wants the children to come to love and appreciate the business.

The two situations may look similar. But the purpose of the second visit is very different from the purpose of the first. In the first situation, it's an exercise in entitlement—"I can do anything I want because it's my family's business." In the second, it's an attempt to enable children to earn respect and to develop appropriate roles in the business. The second wife is part of a family that invests in the younger family members out of concern for succession. Sometimes, you'll find spouses, male or female, of each type within the same family—and not just at the CEO level.

Lastly, suppose a family manufactures kitchen cabinets and emphasizes producing only the best quality, high-end cabinetry. What happens when there's a downturn in the economy and the market for top-level cabinetry declines? The company may have to shift its strategy to survive. It might, for example, have to produce lower-priced products and skip some of the high-end features and detailing that built its reputation. That may seem like sacrilege to some of the long-term employees, and there may be some acrimonious, internal debates about what the family and the company stands for. Perhaps the solution finally agreed upon is to provide the best quality cabinetry in a lower-priced market. That enables the family to be consistent with its value of quality, but in a new market.

These examples demonstrate the fact that you can expect quirks and inconsistencies in the business you work for. Expect some confusion at times. Things will not always be as they seem. You will want to look beneath the surface to discover what's really going on and the chapters that follow should help you do that.

A family in business needs your patience and understanding and your sense of humor. For the most part, the family wants what's best for the family and the business, and with wisdom and forbearance, you can help the family get where it wants to go.

Ultimately, it's not just the business that enjoys the value that the family brings to it. The customers benefit, the employees benefit, and so does the community. You may find yourself saying, "You know what? This is a better business because it's a family business. Even though I'm not going to be an owner and I'm not part of their family, I've got a lot of opportunity here that might not be available elsewhere."

Chapter 4

When There's Conflict (and There Will Be Conflict!)

Conflict among family members is easily the greatest source of difficulty and discomfort for non-family employees. Who wants to be around when brothers and sisters are battling with one another, the parents are fighting with their adult children, one branch of the family is at odds with another branch or family shareholders outside the business have declared war on those who work in it? **But conflict is normal and can be healthy when it's addressed. It also serves a purpose, bringing issues into the open and giving family members an opportunity to resolve differences.** Sometimes conflict acts as a warning bell, alerting the family that a course of action needs to be altered.

In this chapter, you will find different ways to respond to conflict in the family, as well as a discussion of some typical causes of conflict. However, conflict is a very complex matter and a thorough discussion of it is beyond the scope of this book. To increase your knowledge so that you can make an even greater contribution to your workplace, we encourage you to read *Conflict and Communication in the Family Business* by Joseph H. Astrachan, Ph.D., and Kristi S. McMillan.

WAYS YOU CAN RESPOND TO CONFLICT

In our experience, there are six "profiles" that describe the way non-family employees respond to family conflict. Some are legitimate, helpful responses, depending on the nature of the conflict, who's involved, and the strength of established relationships. Others aren't helpful at all or, worse, are actually destructive not only to the family but also to the non-family employee. Later in the chapter, when we discuss common conflicts, you will see how some of these responses can be put into use.

Here are the profiles of responses to conflict that we have identified in working with family businesses over the years:

1. **The Victim.** Self-sacrificing victims unwittingly let themselves get trapped into taking sides in the family battles. You saw an example in Chapter 1, when the son complained bitterly about his CEO father to the non-family CFO and the CFO spoke on the son's behalf to the CEO at a cost of his good relationship with the CEO. It's a normal thing to complain to someone else, but it's devastating to employees caught between two family members.

2. **The Shuttle Diplomat.** This person serves as a buffer between two family members but does not take sides. He listens to the complainer and encourages the individual to try to see the matter from the viewpoint of the one he's complaining about. To a daughter who is angry because she thinks her father doesn't trust her, The Shuttle Diplomat might reframe the conflict, saying, "What you might think about before you go see him again is this. He's 67 years old. He's put his life into this company. His parents lived through the Depression and they taught him to conserve cash. So it may not be that he doesn't trust you. It may be that he's just really, really concerned about the extent of the investment that you want to make."

Or the Shuttle Diplomat may offer to help without taking sides: "You know what? I might be able to get your dad to understand you a little better. Do you mind if I talk to him about our conversation? Maybe I can get him to be more flexible."

Sometimes the Shuttle Diplomat serves as a go-between. Suppose two brothers have owned a business for many years, despite an inability to get along together. The business survives because a skilled non-family employee acts as a negotiator between them to get decisions made.

3. The Sponge. This can actually be a very valuable role. Within the business, the Sponge is a non-family employee who lets a family member vent. The Sponge doesn't take any action. She just listens. That allows the family member to get what's troubling him out of his system and enables him to go on for a while.

4. Houdini. When a conflict arises, Houdini-like non-family employees simply disappear. They take cover and decline to be involved. It's a very effective coping mechanism and may be just exactly what the family needs. The Houdini response eliminates the potential for the non-family employee to get caught in the trap of taking sides and drawing the fire of opposing family members. More important, it forces the conflict back into the family's lap to be resolved.

The Houdini response might **not** be the best choice if the conflict is just a matter of misunderstanding that could be cleared up quickly, or if the non-family employee is especially skillful at reframing arguments or negotiating. But when the employee lacks such skills or doesn't have the temperament to cope with conflict, disappearing can be the right thing to do. If such an employee tries to help, he just might make matters worse.

5. The Situational Mentor. Suppose Dan threatens to quit because his dad has rejected what Dan thinks is an important idea. "Dad is so controlling," Dan declares. "He treats me like a kid and he doesn't trust me. I'll never get anywhere here."

The non-family employee can seize the situation as an opportunity to mentor the young man. "Rather than quit," she can say, "maybe what you can do is present a plan for your idea at the next management meeting—not just a 'trust me' plan, but one that includes a business plan complete with financial projections. Let him know in advance that you're doing your homework. Maybe you could even recruit one or two other folks, with your dad's approval, to participate in putting the plan together."

If Dan is acting immature, the Situational Mentor might be able to point that out in a tactful way, suggesting that he won't be taken seriously if he doesn't act in a business-like fashion.

One caution: non-family employees must have high "political capital"—that is, an excellent relationship with the family— before they take on a mentoring role. Otherwise, it can go badly. ("How dare you side with Dan and tell him to give me a business plan on that cockamamie idea! He'll go to a lot of trouble, I won't like it and things between us will be worse!") We talk more about mentoring and political capital in Chapter 11.

6. **The Agitator.** Agitators are people who enjoy playing power games and exacerbating conflict. They usually side with the parent and intensify disagreement among other family members or between the parent and child. Agitators recognize their own power to stir up trouble and often seem to do it just because they want to see a show. They can do enormous harm in a family firm.

These are the most typical options that non-family employees choose when faced with family conflict. Does your own style fit one of these profiles? Many non-family employees alternate between several roles, depending on the situation.

Reframing: An Excellent Tool

"Reframing" means restating a conflict or an argument so that it changes the context and gives new perspective to a situation. For example, a father may be very angry that his 33-year-old son wants to have increased control in a family business. A skilled non-family executive might ask the father, "Now, what were you doing when you were 33?" The question causes the father to pause. "I took over the company when I was 30," he finally answers. "I was running it when I was 33."

Now the father has a new perspective on his son's desire for more control. If the father was already running the company at 33, why isn't it reasonable for the son to want more control?

Reframing can help people see things in a different light and soften their attitudes so that they listen to each other and understand each other better.

CAUSES OF CONFLICT—AND WAYS TO HELP

In our consulting work, we see five common sources of conflict in family businesses. Here's what they are and some suggestions for how you can be of help. It's critical for you to understand that these suggestions offer only a starting point. Our hope is that they will stimulate your thinking and creativity so that you can come up with solutions and responses that are the most appropriate to your situation. And as you think about your role, please remember our most important rule, which is to **first, do no harm!**

1. Difficulty Separating Family Issues from Business Issues

Take another look at the three-circle model on page 12. It will refresh your memory about how roles in a family business overlap and how some family members might play just one role while others play two, three, or all roles.

One of the most frequently reported conflicts in family businesses concerns compensation. Business-owning families often get stuck between wanting to operate as a family in which everyone is compensated equally, or operating as a business in which the merit system applies and different positions garner different kinds of salaries and rewards. Suppose you have two siblings in the business, Carrie and Wayne. Carrie, the younger of the two, is an excellent salesperson. She is critical of Wayne's performance and believes she contributes much more to the business and is deserving of higher pay. Her view is that "pay should be a function of merit and the contribution of the job." However, Wayne, who is in production, believes that "pay is a function of family status." What's more, Wayne has told his mother, the CEO, how he feels. "I am unhappy that Carrie earns more money than me. I thought you and dad wanted us to share in things equally."

In this case, compensation quickly becomes a difficult issue for both the children and parents.

Consider another scenario that directly affects you, the non-family employee. Suppose you work in a business where family employees are not bound by the compensation system that applies to the rest of the employees, and Alex, a young family member, works for you. Alex has two siblings in the business and their father has just given them all a $15,000 raise. Dad's reasoning is that his children are moving forward in their lives and careers. They're getting married and starting families. They need more money. It gets complicated because Alex's extra $15,000 is coming out of your department's budget, an expenditure you hadn't planned on.

In each of these cases, the family has not resolved the issue of whether to reward family members based on merit and position or based on their family status.

Of course, there are other situations where the family has difficulty separating business from family that aren't centered on compensation. An older brother, Josh, has been in the company for ten years, ever since he got a bachelor's degree. He has been moving up the corporate ladder steadily. His younger brother, Mort, puts time and effort into earning an M.B.A. and then getting some solid experience with other companies. Not long after Mort finally joins the family firm, he comes to the conclusion that his older brother, Josh, is on the path to being chosen as the next leader and that he is not even being considered. In a conversation with one of the non-family employees, he complains that all his credentials are being disregarded. "I'm more qualified. I've got this degree. I've got valuable experience outside the company."

What You Can Do. Begin with two critical steps. Empathize with the family and the difficult problems it faces. At the same time, understand what's really going on. In the last scenario, Mort offers all the *business* reasons why he should be considered for the top job, but what's really on his mind is, "I don't want to work for my older brother." What appears to be a business issue is, in fact, a family issue. Mort has probably seen the leadership style of his father as one of a dictator and he's thinking, "Now my brother gets to be dictator. How can I live with that?"

Back to the compensation example, part of empathizing with the family is to resist forming an opinion too quickly, such as that "everybody should be paid on merit." The businesses described above are making a transition from an owner/manager to two or more siblings. It's common at this stage, while the business is still relatively young and small, to compensate siblings equally. When the business is a large, fifth-generation corporation, compensation based on merit is essential, but the family and business aren't there yet. It helps to understand what stage of development the business is in and what is typical for that stage. We'll get into that beginning with the next chapter.

More specifically, you should *tactfully* and *nonjudgmentally* begin to encourage the family to develop policies that will help them separate family issues from business issues and establish expectations for family members with regard to their participation in and compensation from the family enterprise. If you have a good relationship with the family, you might say something like: "We have somewhat of an awkward situation here in that we've got two different compensation systems—one for family and one for non-family. Is that a question the owners wish to take on? Should we treat family employees differently than non-family? The other managers and I see this as an issue for the family to decide. It's not really ours to say."

If you're that manager whose family employee just got the $15,000 raise, you may need to use a velvet-covered brick and ask the family how it expects you to meet your departmental goals now that this additional expenditure has been added. It's the kind of question a family has to wrestle with for itself, but it's on your budget so you have a right to inquire—as long as you use lots of velvet. You can also help by making sure that the family employee you are overseeing knows what the performance goals and expectations are and gets accurate, objective feedback on how he or she is doing. We should note here that even families who do embrace market-based compensation for family employees may often pay them from a separate budget regardless of their assignment.

In the case of Mort, who does not want to work for his brother, you can suggest to the family that they deal with three things: (1) developing a *process* for selection of the next leader rather than focusing on *who* it's going to be; (2) determining what the standard for leadership will be—leadership by consensus? By committee? Another dictatorship? (3) designing a career path for the younger brother so he can see how he can fit into the organization and contribute in a meaningful way.

2. Communication Difficulties that Result from Overlaying the Family System on the Business System

When family and business roles blur, communication often locks up.

"Honor your father and mother" might be an important part of the family code. In the business, however, that can get translated into, "Whatever you do, don't question Mom and Dad." Not questioning parents in the business environment, however, may be dangerous from a strategic standpoint if other family members perceive a bet-the-farm decision being made by Dad is without input from family, key employees, or advisors.

In another example, Dad may be seen by the family as the protector and caretaker for the children. But he so values that role that he continues to fill it when the children come into the business, and they continue to let him. He protects them and provides for them and promises to take care of them. The sons and daughters can't have an honest discussion with him about their salaries and other matters because he has always taken care of them and to do so would question dad's intentions. So they can't ask for a raise, inquire about estate planning, or raise any sensitive subject.

In still another case, the family so values harmony that its way of dealing with conflict is to avoid it. As the children grow up and join their parents in the business, the family continues to avoid conflict. As a result, they can't question or even discuss business strategy because there might be a disagreement.

And one more example: Mom is the CEO of the family business. Her son and daughter have been vying for her attention as a mother ever since they were small. Now as adults in the business, they're still fighting for her attention. In doing so, they have become very competitive and have a hard time demonstrating teamwork. Mom gets fed up and "silos" her offspring, giving her son one set of businesses to run and her daughter another. The siblings rarely have to talk to each other. The family issue of a brother and a sister trying to win the attention of the parent has turned into the reality that the siblings can't work together well in the business.

What You Can Do. One way to help the family owners is to predict the future as a means of getting the family's attention and making them aware that they have to deal with the situation directly. In the last example, you might say to the family, "You know, if this silo style of dealing with family members continues, it's likely that there will be a blowup as soon as Mom retires."

Again, it's essential to be nonjudgmental. Aim to offer solutions rather than approach the family with an attitude that says "you're the problem." In the case of the business where the children feel they can't question Mom or Dad, you might approach the parents and call their attention to the pattern you've observed. You can point out that many successful families rely on the senior generation to teach the younger family members how to stand up and effectively present their ideas about where they see the business going. You might say, "One of the things I've noticed is that the kids seem to be afraid to bring issues up. In my experience, a healthy organization is one where the employees are bringing new ideas to the table even if they're somewhat controversial, as long as they've done their homework. What can we do to get the junior generation to step up to the plate?"

Or you might reframe the discussion and say, "Having the junior generation know how to present strategy is a way for family leadership continuity to occur, and I'd like to help you get the junior generation ready."

3. Equal Opportunity versus Equal Outcome

Another conflict-producing situation occurs when one or more members of the family insist on equal outcomes for all the younger-generation family members. This has a particularly strong effect on the sibling generation. Typically, an overly protective mother insists that all her kids succeed. In her view, if one gets a promotion, then the others have to get promotions as well, even if they're not performing adequately.

The mother's motives are laudable. She wants equal success for all her children, and she believes equal outcomes for all will produce harmony. Instead, the situation usually results in high-level conflict among the siblings. Those who truly earned a promotion end up being angry at those who were promoted just because they were family members. You, the non-family employee, may get caught up in a strange series of promotions of family members, or the awarding of company perks to a family member for no apparent reason.

What You Can Do. First, understand that it's not your problem. Now might be a good time to play Houdini. Approach it the same way you would approach someone having an unresolved conflict: don't go too far. You may offer a suggestion when you're asked, or you may suggest lightly without judging and without the need for a response. But you'll find yourself in a real trap if you pursue that issue as though it's yours to solve.

If you have a solid standing with the family, however, and the opportunity presents itself, you can bring a lot of value to the family by asking, "Could you look at this as equal in terms of opportunity rather than equal in terms of outcome? You won't be able to manage the outcome forever."

4. Differing Expectations

As a family business grows older and larger and there are more family shareholders, people are more likely to have differing expectations about such matters as where the firm is going, accountability and responsibility, financial rewards, advancement, and decision making. By the time you get to the cousin generation, the number of people involved makes it harder to come to agreement on the direction of the business. Different family members may begin to form different expectations about how much risk the business ought to take on, whether it's a stewardship responsibility or an investment. Unless expectations are managed successfully, the family can erupt in conflict so severe that it ruins the business or the business is sold.

What You Can Do. If you have the ability and if you have sufficient standing with the family, you can seize the opportunity to play Situational Mentor to the whole family. First, you'll want to assure the family that what they're going through is a normal cycle—nearly every family business experiences this kind of turmoil. You can point out that a business-owning family that never goes through this kind of mismatched expectation may actually be sliding toward destruction because the issues don't get raised.

Then you can point out that it's the family's responsibility to develop a system for making decisions and to find a way for everyone to be heard in the process—not just older family managers and shareholders, but the in-laws and the future shareholders. You may want to encourage the family to bring in a consultant to help them develop a decision-making process.

If you lack the political capital and the skills to act as a family mentor here, it's best perhaps to be Houdini and disappear or be The Sponge and just respectfully listen.

5. Dealing with Feelings about Change

There will be some anxiety as people shift roles. A daughter who is advancing rapidly may want a greater voice in company decisions, while her parent may feel discomfort about giving her more of a say. Their pull and tug may turn into conflict.

The CEO or other senior-generation managers will have mixed emotions as they move toward retirement. Their desire to stay on the job may be at odds with the desire to let the next generation come to power, and most senior leaders have some reservations about what life will be like when they are no longer in the company. Their ambiguity will lead them to experience many ups and downs, exhibiting observable emotional swings along the way.

As younger family members become shareholders, they may feel like they should have more of a voice than they actually get. This becomes another source of antagonism.

In extreme (but not uncommon) situations, senior-generation leaders may become so entrenched in their role that they refuse to even discuss transition. Their emotions about the matter may be so strong that letting go is out of the question. They may say things like, "I am never going to retire and you are just going to have to live with it." Junior-generation leaders may begin to question whether they will ever have a chance to contribute to or control their own destiny.

All of these situations will set off uneasy feelings of "What is the appropriate behavior here?"

What You Can Do. Again, all the above scenarios are normal and predictable. Family members are just trying to work out difficult feelings and they'll need some time to do so. You might serve best here as The Sponge or Houdini, keeping a low profile and trusting that those involved will eventually gain clarity in their roles and expectations. In the extreme example where an entrenched senior leader refuses to relinquish power, listening is of utmost importance. Venting allows both generations to handle this stressful situation. If the relationship between the senior and junior generation worsens, you may recommend that the family consult with a family business specialist. A specialist can help the family better understand the situation and how to cope with it. In some cases, when the tension is too great, it may be best if "junior" leaves the company and pursues other opportunities. This message, however, is usually best delivered by an outsider, who has no conflicting interests in advising the family and can help the family move forward.

A REAL OPPORTUNITY

It's important to remember that while conflicts make the work environment uncomfortable, every family has conflicts. If you leave the company you work for now and join another family-owned firm, you'll find conflict there, as well.

Instead, look at the family's conflicts as genuine opportunities to be of service and increase your value as a non-family employee. When you have the ear of family members, you can ask the kinds of questions that enable and encourage them to work through contentious issues. You can suggest areas that need work, and you can point out that there's a body of family business knowledge that the family can take advantage of—be it through seminars, books, and publications or consultation. You may also find a family business center at your local university. You can contribute, too, by increasing your own knowledge of the environment in which you work. The following chapters will help you do that. The more you know the better position you'll be in to support the family in its difficult task of combining family and business.

Chapter 5

Difficult Passage #1

From a Founder to Sons and Daughters

How you handle your role as a non-family employee in a family business is going to depend on a number of factors. Among the most important are the circumstances confronting the business and the owning family's priorities related to family and business. This chapter introduces the first of five family business profiles: (1) a business in transition from a founder (or founding parents) to a son, daughter, or a sibling team; (2) a business in transition from a sibling team to a group of cousins; (3) a "family-first" business; (4) a "business-first" business; and (5) a family business in crisis or facing impending crisis. A family business at any stage—founder, sibling partnership, or cousin group—can be characterized as "family first" or "business first," or can strike a balance between the two. And, a family at any stage, no matter what its orientation, can be in crisis. These pages are aimed at helping you to analyze and understand what kind of business you are in and what it may be going through. In each chapter, you will also find ideas for what you can do to help and, in some cases, traps to avoid.

IS THIS BUSINESS AT RISK?

Succession of a family business from one generation to the next can be so tumultuous that it seems like a crisis. The parents are struggling with their children and the children are battling one another. You have your own reservations about the abilities of the children and how prepared they are to take over leadership. You may worry that the business is at risk and start wondering if you should be looking for another job. But stay calm. In most cases, what you see happening is actually quite normal.

When a business undergoes a transition from a founder to the next generation, differing but very natural perspectives influence the process. (For the sake of simplicity here, we'll use such terms as "founder" or "senior generation." A founder might also be a husband and wife team or other partners.) Because the senior and junior generations are at such different stages in their lives, what one is trying to accomplish contrasts markedly from what the other hopes to achieve. They each have many separate needs and desires. Exhibit 4 illustrates some of these differences.

Despite these disparities, there are four things that each generation wants: a winning strategy, strong leadership, a voice in what happens, and financial performance.

It's a natural part of the development process that young people try to differentiate themselves from their parents. In a family business, this may mean younger family members trying to introduce more formality and professionalism into business management, organizing their own management team, and navigating between loyalties to their parent and their emerging loyalties to the new leadership team.

When there are multiple siblings involved, succession becomes even more complicated as sibling conflict and competition issues are introduced. What's more, some siblings may work in the business while others, although owners, do not. All are trying to sort out their different roles.

The founder may want the company to continue as a family business, but struggle with the idea of letting go of

EXHIBIT 4   How Seniors and Juniors Differ

Seniors	Juniors
Want to protect their investment and their cash flow by being conservative.	Want to protect their investment and their cash flow by not being too conservative.
Seek to be loyal to key employees.	Seek accountability for all employees.
Want to feel useful and not lose too much control.	Want to feel in control.
Want to be secure in retirement.	Want to live a financially comfortable life, as they have been.
Want to preserve family harmony.	Want to focus on the business.
Want to think about (or avoid thinking about!) life outside the business.	Are immersed in building a career inside the business.
Take pride in the strategy that has worked in the past.	Want to take pride in their own strategy.
Want to be seen as important.	Want to be seen as leaders.
Want to "harvest" the business.	Want to reinvest in the business.
Say, "Show me."	Say, "Trust me."

control—particularly if the sons and daughters are in conflict. (For a thorough discussion of owners at this stage of life, please see *Letting Go: Preparing Yourself to Relinquish Control of the Family Business* by Craig E. Aronoff, Ph.D.

There are four things that each generation wants:
a winning strategy, strong leadership, a voice in
what happens, and financial performance.

WHAT YOU CAN DO

Here are some steps you can take to help the family business and
protect yourself as the family contends with this particular succession transition:

Enhance Trust among the Siblings. The more they trust each
other, the less they will fight. One way you can help is by following protocol and being transparent about your actions. When
one son asks for assistance, your natural inclination will be to
help. But you have to keep in mind how being helpful to one
sibling will be perceived by the others. If you are asked to provide information to a sibling-owner who's not employed in the
business, for example, it's wise to refer the request to the individual, family or non-family (often the founder), in charge of communication with shareholders. When you adhere to protocol,
your actions are much easier for all to observe. The siblings see
that you are not going behind anyone's back, and your actions
become less likely to serve as a new source of conflict or diminish
trust among the siblings.

Foster Teamwork among the Siblings. We have known non-
family employees who have taken the members of the younger
generation aside and said, "This business could be yours someday. It's important for you to communicate with one another.
Why don't we go out to lunch and just talk about it sometime?"
In that way, such managers launch a series of sessions in which
the young family members talk about preparing themselves as a
group of leaders.
     Another effective way to inspire teamwork is to set an exam-
ple. That happens when non-family employees do a better job of

teaming among themselves. You don't have to wait for the family to "get its act together" for good things to happen in the business. There are some initiatives you can take, and when you and the other employees bridge your own gaps and work together more effectively, you are showing the whole family, not just the siblings, how to work as a team.

Encourage Accountability. Generally, most second-generation leaders want more accountability in the business, so they're likely to be receptive to your efforts to help. You can encourage accountability not just in your own department but throughout the company, and not just with non-family employees but with family employees as well. Be active in helping family employees think through their job descriptions, goals, and measurements of success. Young family members at the sibling level in particular are going to be looking at one another and asking the question, "How are we performing?" "What do we need to learn?" "How can we assume more responsibility?" You can play a role in nurturing that accountability mindset.

Again, you can network with other non-family employees to encourage an environment of accountability throughout the company. Understand, however, that the move from a system based on loyalty to one based on accountability presents some prickly issues. Older non-family employees who have worked with Dad for decades may resist this change. Consider a man we'll call Blake. He's a key non-family department head who has been working with Lew, the 62-year-old founder and CEO, for 25 years. The two men have a great deal of loyalty toward each other. Now Lew's children are rising in the business and, in their efforts to introduce accountability and professionalism, they are asking Blake for more information than he has ever provided to anyone but Lew. According to Blake, Lew has always kept this information confidential, and Blake is reluctant to disclose information beyond what Lew wants. Indeed, there's general resistance from Lew to move toward "professional management." Lew's resistance is further reinforced by Blake and other non-family employees who don't want to move in that direction, either.

But time marches on and, ultimately, the younger generation comes to power. What we have observed is that non-family employees who are resistant to change eventually come to be seen as impediments to change, even deadwood, and they often lose their jobs or influential roles under new leadership.

It needn't be that way. Non-family employees who recognize that they have been adhering to a "loyalty is everything" culture and start shifting to "loyalty and accountability" are going to increase their value to the organization and help it make the changes that must be made if the firm is going to be successful in the future. Rule of thumb: if you are embracing or leading change, you are increasing your value to the firm. If you are fighting change, you may be endangering your future.

Preparing the Successor. One of the most important jobs of key non-family employees is preparing young family members for future leadership roles, particularly that of successor to the CEO. Non-family employees may be asked to assume this role; or they may volunteer for it. It may be an informal process characterized by setting an example, or it may be much more formal, entailing a plotted-out career development program and mentoring or coaching. Whatever the case, it's a serious responsibility and one that is extremely valuable in enabling the family business to move to next-generation leadership.

Rule of thumb: if you are embracing or leading change, you are increasing your value to the firm.

At Monsen Engineering Co. in Fairfield, New Jersey, two key non-family employees initiated the mentoring. In the mid-1990s, Gene Savettiere and Joe Coyle were concerned that without a plan to prepare the owner's son for leadership, succession wouldn't happen. They approached Dick Monsen, the company's 59-year-old president, and shared with him their concerns. Eric Monsen, then 29, was excellent at sales and marketing but had no management experience and lacked the technical sophistication of his father. Dick Monsen listened, and soon, a ten-year program was launched to groom Eric for the presidency. It involved a mentoring team that included Dick Monsen, Savettiere, Coyle, and an outside executive coach. They embarked on a flexible plan that made the most of Eric's gregarious personality and networking and motivational skills, and provided him with experience in management, including union contract negotiations.[12] Dick Monsen has since retired and Eric has succeeded him as president.

Encourage Appropriate Communication. Founders and their spouses can be secretive about company finances, estate plans and business decisions. As the company and family grow and professionalize, a greater flow of information is needed. You may be in a position to encourage the parents to share more information—perhaps by asking them what kind of company performance information they need to keep tabs on the business as the next generation assumes more responsibility. You can also coach the younger generation to provide adequate reporting not only to key managers in the company but also to family shareholders outside the company. You can help them understand that in the long run, they need the support of fellow shareholders and providing them with sufficient information about the company is a good start.

Help Family Members Understand that Things Are Normal. Dad's retired from his New England business and he's gone to Florida. But wait! All of a sudden, he's back, sticking his nose into things and undoing some of his children's decisions. Then he's gone again, and four months later, here he is again.

We call this the "yo-yo" effect and we see it all the time. For the most part, retirement does not mean a founder has made a clean break. More often, founders go into semi-retirement. It's a common reality, and younger family members and employees are best advised to learn to tolerate it and learn to make the best of it. Unless Mom and Dad are being truly destructive, other family members can empathize with them and indulge them a little. The parents are entering a phase of their lives for which they have few guidelines and they can use some understanding and support.

Protect Yourself. We talked earlier about the need to follow protocol and be transparent about your actions. That not only enhances trust among the siblings but also protects you from appearing devious.

Other situations will occur, however, which will put you on the spot. Suppose semi-retired Dad goes to Florida and while he's gone, his newly minted CEO daughter tells you that she's decided to spend $50,000 on updated computer equipment. She knows he doesn't support such a move, so she wants to take action while he is gone. You know that as soon as he finds out, he will return in a fury and a lot of that fury will be aimed directly at you because you didn't let him know what his daughter was doing.

No doubt about it. You're going to be in harm's way.

One thing you can do is to slow down the younger family member by walking her through the consequences of the decision. Tell her what you think is likely to happen. Ask, "How are you going to make sure that this doesn't become a problem for future decisions that you want to make or future plans that you want to implement?" It's also legitimate to point out to her the position she's putting you in and to ask: "How are you going to protect me?"

Traps to Avoid

1. Choosing to side with one generation or the other. If you choose the senior generation, there will likely be no place for you in the business when the next generation takes over. If you side with the younger family members, Mom or Dad may fire you.

   You can be loyal to both generations by serving the whole family and doing what's best for the business. Taking a long-range view will help.

2. Emphasizing your past loyalties in hopes of avoiding difficult change. Your past loyalties are appreciated and have placed you in a position to achieve results toward new strategic challenges. Focus on accountability of yourself and those you supervision.

3. Underpreparing the successor. When a successor is not really ready to lead, that leaves the company open for the retired parent to come back and "rescue" the company. It's a situation that stalls succession.

Chapter 6

Difficult Passage #2

From Sibling Control to
Next-Generation Cousins

In this transition, the junior generation consists of the young cousins who are now coming into a sibling-owned business. Many situations may cause hard feelings to develop. Suppose I am the son or daughter of a sibling who did not work in the business but who is an owner. I don't work in the business, either, because my parent didn't. But my cousins are in the business, in cushy jobs, being paid high salaries, and getting all kinds of special treatment. At least, that's my perception. It's natural for me to be annoyed or envious or even angry that no one ever thought I might have an interest in working in the business that my grandfather or great-grandfather started.

Or suppose that my grandparents decided that only those who work in the business could be substantial shareholders. My two uncles got to work in the business because they were males and were considered more appropriate. Together, they control the business. My mother ended up being a nurse and received a very minor holding in the business. Even though my grandparents left her a generous inheritance outside the business, the business has made my uncles extremely wealthy and my family's lifestyle has been very modest compared to my cousins'. It is understandable that I may have hard feelings over the situation.

Or maybe I'm the sibling who is now CEO. Three of my children work in the business with me. We all work long, stressful hours to continue making this business a success. My siblings and, increasingly, my nieces and nephews, earn dividends from our hard work, but all they do is complain. They haven't a clue as to how difficult our jobs are.

It's not possible to go through all the permutations of what a family business looks like at this stage, but you get the picture. It's complicated and there may be many emotional land mines—some of which you, as a non-family employee, will have to dodge.

As a cousin, living in the same community as the business, I may feel like I'm in a fishbowl. It may seem as though my every move is scrutinized because I belong to this well-known family who owns this well-known business.

The family is also now more dispersed. Some family shareholders have moved to other parts of the country where they have jobs outside of the family business. There are more and more in-laws who bring influences from their own individual personalities and family cultures. It's harder to bring family members together. Some of the cousins don't even know each other.

On a positive note, the business is becoming larger and more professionalized. The family may see the establishment of an independent board of directors as an enhancement. They may be moving from a sibling partnership to an organization where there's a clear, single leader.

Department heads are making more of an impact now. More than ever before, there are important jobs for non-family employees to fill. Consequently, non-family employees have opportunities for greater influence.

WHAT YOU CAN DO

Many of the things suggested in the preceding chapter apply here as well. You can work to enhance trust, foster teamwork, and encourage communication but now among cousins as well as siblings. You will also be needed just as much as before to support an environment of accountability.

As the business moves from the hands of the siblings to the cousins, however, there are contributions specific to the transition that you might be in a position to make. For example, you could:

Foster Trust between Branches of the Family. If you're the CFO, you can help the family managers think through the question, "What information do we want to share with your inactive cousin shareholders to help them understand this business and how can we encourage their support?" With your help, family members in the business will come to see that inactive shareholders not only want regular, meaningful financial reporting but also enjoy being kept up to date on exciting new developments, like the acquisition of state-of-the-art machinery, the introduction of innovative products or services, or recognition the company has won for accomplishments that reflect the family's values.

You can assist insiders in seeing that treating minority shareholders with respect works to secure their commitment to the business, while isolating them only fuels resentment that leads to a desire to redeem their shares or sell the business altogether. You can instill the notion that the outside cousins' support also enables the inside cousins to stay focused on their jobs and move the business forward. Perhaps you can also help family managers see that good shareholder relations can even result in the outside cousins foregoing a special dividend so that the business can make an important investment.

Help the Family See the Importance of Taking Steps Now to Nurture Good Relationships among the Cousins that Will Be Invaluable 10 or 20 Years from Now. When they understand that the business is going to be owned by a group of cousins, families on the leading edge put a great deal of effort into activities that will enhance relationships and encourage unity among the cousins. They start when the cousins are as young as 10, engaging them in group discussions, having fun together via family vacations, family meetings, or other events.

But not all business-owning families have such foresight. If you're in a strong enough position to guide the family in this direction, you will be performing an incredibly valuable, long-term service for the family and the business. When cousins have good relationships, extended family members are more likely to see themselves as part of one family rather than as part of one branch seeking only what is best for that branch. As shareholders, they will find it easier to speak with one voice.

Train Individual Family Members Who Will Not Be the Future CEO. As the business grows larger and more family members join it, they will need to develop skills to fill important jobs below the CEO level. You can help them acquire those skills and learn to take pride in their own individual performance, as well as help them develop the emotional intelligence needed to succeed in their own right, without depending on the business. A non-family employee can also encourage younger family members to adopt a stewardship mentality that will help assure the continuity of the business.

Encourage Protocol. Help the adult siblings see the value of developing family employment policies before the cousins are ready to join the business. Urge them to have discussions about compensation and about who supervises and reviews who well before the cousins graduate from school and become employees. When you encourage clear protocol and conformance to it, you help prevent many headaches, and heartaches, down the road.

Help the Family See the Bigger Picture. Assist family members in understanding the value of the family to the business. As opportunities arise, help the family see the long-term consequences of actions taken or not taken today. You might point out to the CEO that it would be wise to invite her teenage niece or nephew from several states away to spend the summer working in the business, just as her children do. You might point out that the business could benefit from some extraordinary future talent by including those children. If you have the ear of the senior family leaders, you might remind them of the value their voice has brought to the business, and encourage them to integrate younger family employees into that "voice" so as to continue a great legacy of family leadership.

Traps to Avoid

1. Getting caught between family branches. You may see two branches vying for advantages for their children—for promotions, for example, or better pay and bigger perks. Just as you should not side with one generation or another, do not align yourself with one branch of the family.

   Learn to navigate well between the family's branches, and between those who work in the business and those who do not. Follow protocol and make your own actions as transparent as possible.

2. Aligning yourself with one cousin against another, even though you think one of them has a legitimate point or complaint. Empathize. Be The Sponge. Play Houdini, if you have to. Or turn the problem back to the family, asking the complainant, "How can you work within your family in order to get this addressed in a way that is going to be most successful for your family relationships as well as for this business?"

3. Getting locked into the notion that a particular cousin is the obvious successor and giving that person 100 percent of your attention. Doing so has the potential for isolating that person from meeting the needs of the family, fostering in him a sense that he's right and he doesn't have to consider his siblings or cousins. This leads to destructiveness in the business and, if this cousin doesn't become CEO, potential risk to your career.

Chapter 7

Understanding a "Family-First" Business

Family business consultants have found it useful to understand whether the business we are working with is a "family-first" business or a "business-first" business. You may find that thinking about the company you work for in these terms is helpful to you, too. Let's begin with family-first businesses.

A family-first company is one whose owners tend to think that providing employment and other advantages to family members is one of the primary purposes of the enterprise. Having all the kids working together in the business represents success to this family. The business' performance is of course important, but hitting on all eight cylinders all the time is secondary to employing the new son-in-law, even though his training and experience don't fit the business at all. He's joined the family; he's got a job. Often, the failures of individual family employees may be viewed as learning experiences that don't necessarily require a lot of follow-up.

"Our company is a much stronger company because we have so much family involved," these families say. They believe that the family's values are the right values to make the business a success. Out of that belief, they fill all the key positions with family members. As a result, the business's strategy, management, and finances are influenced by the number of family members in the business and their skills and interests.

Suppose a family owns a grocery business with three stores. Dad, the founder, is the CEO. Mom is the COO, overseeing the front office, human resources, and customer service. Son Joey heads the meat department. His sister, Meg, runs produce. Two other brothers and Meg's husband each manage one of the stores. The business provides a good living for the family and its employees. More important, it serves the core purpose of giving family members the opportunity to work together running a business the way they feel is best and earning a good living at it.

A family-first business can work well in a protected niche environment—that is, when competition is not so fierce that the company is forced to move toward pure accountability. Some of the most successful family-first businesses are those that provide an "experience" for customers, or where customer service is a major factor. Good examples are restaurants where the family members are front and center, yet it could also be the supplier to the restaurant and many more like it, where relationships are key. They know the customers and make them feel at home. The collective family is a key part of what makes such businesses successful.

You probably know of some family farms that have expanded and diversified, evolving perhaps into a cluster of businesses, including a pick-your-own operation, a restaurant featuring "home cooking," hayrides and other entertainment, a country gift shop, a produce market, a Christmas shop, and perhaps a petting zoo. The founding parents' children and some in-laws probably each run a major facet of the operation, and perhaps there's a non-family employee or two to handle positions that family members are ill-equipped to manage—such as a controller. Or there may be one "star" non-family employee who has been with the company since he was a college student and has been, in a way, "adopted" by the family. For the most part, people in the senior positions are probably not paid what they're really worth, but because most of them are family, they're willing to sacrifice a lot more than non-family employees might for the same positions.

Non-family employees can have a great deal of fun in such a business and will most likely enjoy the "we're all family" environment. But they're also going to see that all the key spots are filled by family members. Essentially, there's little or no opportunity for upward advancement. If you have your heart set on running a business someday, this may not be the place for you. What's more, it may be clear that the business is not going to adopt professional management practices over time the way another business might. It's less likely to be performance-oriented than other companies and less likely to be on the cutting edge. That is not the strategy of a family-first organization. Family-first companies that value relationships over capabilities may have a blind spot.

Consider the W. P. Smith Company located in Bakersfield, California. It's a fictitious example, similar to hundreds of family-first firms we know and it will make our point. Customers and employees might identify this company as a family-first business, yet contrasted with family firms on that end of the continuum, they do not put family first in all respects. They are proud to have their family working with them in this produce processing and distribution business. The four family members in the second generation fill major management positions except the CEO slot. Dave Powers, the non-family CEO says, "In this company we have fun, we all know each others' families, and I am like a big brother to all the younger family members who work here and even the ones who don't. The four brothers meet every week. One issue that I've been discussing with them is that their long-term customers are putting pressure on us for better pricing because our competitors have adopted efficiencies that allow them to beat us." The brothers insist that they will be okay as the customers are long-term friends; and loyalty is what the family stands for. They say the customers fall into the market segment that knows quality service and integrity ultimately saves them money and they are willing to pay more for it. Dave knows this was true in the past, yet he is concerned that the business might need to provide both loyal relationships and better pricing.

WHAT YOU CAN DO

If your company is a family-first organization, chances are you can't expect a more impressive title or an innovative strategic leadership position in the marketplace. Still, there are some tactics you can choose to advance your career and assist the business:

Gain Additional Trust, Responsibility, and Compensation— without the Title. Don't push for the limelight and don't compete with a family member for a leadership position. Do, however, ask yourself, "What can I offer to the success of this business from a strategic or tactical standpoint?" Build your knowledge and experience by taking on challenges for which family members lack knowledge, value to the business, or interest. Understand the owning family's goals and values, and act accordingly. Be vigilant to problems that may blindside the family and play a key role in confronting them. Realize that loyalty may be the most highly valued attribute that you can offer.

Speak the family's language instead of expecting the family to speak a new one.

Quietly Initiate Change. Suppose you've been reading up on strategic planning and you know there are some things your company could be doing. Don't demand that the organization adopt professional management practices or change. Don't insist that it meet your standards. Don't even ask permission. Instead, consider what elements of strategic planning can be worked into what the company is already doing. Then, just informally and unobtrusively get the job done. That's the "forgiveness route." Do it, and, if necessary, ask forgiveness later. The key is to work with the flow and help the business accommodate the kinds of advances that fit within its culture and values. Speak the family's language instead of expecting the family to speak a new one.

Recognize that if You're Part of the Business, You Are Part of the Family. When invited to dinner or family events, you and your family are expected to attend. But remember, *their* family should and will get center stage.

Willingly take on the role of helping new family members learn how to adapt and be successful in the business. Encourage others around you to do the same and to focus on the value multiple family members bring to the business. It is all too easy to sit back and take pot shots at the family. Be a leader in discouraging a "we-they" atmosphere among employees.

Traps to Avoid

1. Violating the unwritten rules. Don't try to make changes before you know the rules, but remember different families have different rules so be careful about your own assumptions.

   Rules may be things like (1) don't put the spotlight on a family member's mistakes; (2) don't suggest to the senior generation that a younger family member is in the wrong position; (3) the family members' informal communication with one another is probably their main communication link; recognize that and work with it; (4) you report to the whole family, not just your boss; the family members consider themselves a unit; and (5) poor performance on the part of a family member is not discussable. Other families may expect non-family employees to give young family members firm guidance, or have a patriarch or matriarch who controls the business and the family.

2. Getting too comfortable. Some non-family employees come to feel so cozy and secure in a family-first environment that they fail to notice that the business is headed for disaster. Instead of offering additional value to the company, they collude with the owners in the belief that the owners are the only ones who can bring change.

It's essential to stay on your toes and keep yourself prepared for what the business needs. Continue to ask yourself such questions as: Am I still developing as a person? Am I so comfortable that I do the job that I did yesterday, but I don't think about what job needs to be done tomorrow? What enhancements can I make to this business?

3. Even if your employers say that the business is a big family and even if you come to be treated almost as family, always remember that you are not family and act accordingly.

Chapter 8

What about "Business-First" Companies?

What we described in the last chapter is really a purist view of a family-first company. Most businesses are not as extreme but instead fall somewhere on a continuum between being completely family-first or entirely business-first. Our point is not to help you "fix" the situation but to help you find ways to be effective within it. That said, let's look at some of the characteristics that mark business-first families.

They have a lot in common with public companies. It's hard to even recognize there's a family involved in a business-first business because the family may be so far removed from it. If there are family members in the business, they are granted no special considerations. Family members not employed in the business are accorded no special privileges. Only those members associated with stock ownership have special rights and gain benefit.

This is a company that adheres strictly to business rules. When it comes to advancement and compensation, it operates on a "market and merit" system. You'll probably see few family conflicts in a business-first company because family members distance themselves much more than a family-first family would.

You may hear statements from the family like, "Any family member who's not in the business is not going to own stock."

And, "Only those who are working in the business have a right to influence it." When there are family shareholders who are not employed in the business, they tend to view their ownership as an investment rather than as a legacy or a family heirloom they hope to pass on to their children. Their main interest is return on investment.

In some ways, **business-first companies offer a very desirable situation for non-family employees.** For one thing, they're probably not confronted with intruding family members and their dynamics. For another, if a non-family employee is supervising one of the younger family members, it's a given that the family member is to be treated like anyone else in the company and the employee doesn't have to put up with any "I'm an owner" attitude. It's just business, and the emphasis is on individual and company performance.

In many respects, a business-first company is almost not a family business. While it may be very successful and may seem very attractive to some uninformed non-family employees, it may or may not be a very secure situation for them in the long run. Some enterprises that lean in this direction, such as the New York Times Company, thrive for generation after generation in the control of the same family. Others, however, are sold because family members want independence from one another and seek to liquidate their shares. Sometimes the only way to provide the separation that they're looking for is through a sale.

WHAT YOU CAN DO

Here are some thoughts about what you can do as a non-family employee in the less-personal environment of a business-first company:

◆ **Consider whether you can play a role in demonstrating to the family where it can be of value, as family, to the business.**

This will probably be a surprising message to the family. Perhaps the founder long ago had seen too many businesses fail because of family discord and decided to discourage family involvement. However, you do not automatically need to accept the myth that goes, "An inch of family involvement in the business turns into a mile of unprepared family members feeling entitled to get involved in anything they please, from the work performance of the receptionist to the growth strategy of the business." Many first-class family firms take pride in operating or owning very effective businesses, which play by all the business rules, yet actively include family members and future shareholders in ways that enhance the business and its longevity as a family enterprise.

If you are in a position to do so, you might point out the value of having competent family members well represented in the governance of the business or in key positions in the company. Perhaps you can encourage the family to consider how its values can play a positive role in the business and the benefit to employees if all family members defined one set of values to live by and made them available to management and employees. Many family firms' value and mission statements add to the "heart" and culture of an organization.

You might find that it makes sense to suggest that standards for involvement, and the kind of involvement, be examined by the family so that the message is clear: "The business will be run like a business, yet we will do everything we can to see that serious, qualified family members have opportunities to work in roles where they will make valued contributions." Of perhaps greater value, you can encourage closer connections between the growing body of family shareholders and the business so they begin to see it as more than just an investment. Lacking those connections, ownership continuity may be unlikely.

◆ **Make yourself indispensable and keep your skill sets finely tuned.** This is always good advice. First, you want to make the best contribution you can to your company. Second, you want to stay employable. If your company is sold, you will have a better chance of being kept on by the new owners or finding a new position elsewhere if you have a record as a top performer.

FINDING THE RIGHT BALANCE

Obviously, our bias is toward finding the right balance between being "family-first" and "business-first." Sometimes, a business may need to lean more in one direction than the other, depending on the circumstances. If there's no family member in the next generation competent to serve as CEO, the family would be wise to hire or promote a capable non-family employee for the position. That's a business-first decision in the short run, but in the long-run, it's a family-first decision, too, because it helps assure the survival of the business so that it can be passed on to future generations of family members.

The family employment policy drawn up by the Stoller family at Widmer Interiors offers an excellent example of family-first business-first balance. While it affirms that "a family working together, sharing a common vision can be a powerful and competitive business entity," it lays out the expectations for family members who wish to be employed in the company. They must have a strong work ethic, attain the appropriate education and training, and understand that rewards will be commensurate with the contribution they make.

In keeping with a business-first attitude, family employees are told they will be subject to the same employment policies as non-family employees, and their compensation will generally be the same as that of non-family employees. In a departure that is distinctly "family-first," however, family members' spouses are told that bonuses and perks, if any, will be related to their status as a spouse and "will be distributed equally to all spouses, even if they are not active in the business." The document also tells family spouses that while they are to abide by the same policies as other employees, "some leniency may be granted (e.g., vacation time)."[13]

To our way of thinking, the Stoller family has found a way to appropriately involve family members without compromising sound business practices.

Chapter 9

When Crisis Looms

Often family businesses seem in crisis when they are actually just going through difficult but normal transitions. Family members fighting in the business, an excessive family-first mindset, disgruntled family shareholders—all can make you wonder if the business you work for is about to explode. It probably is not going to.

The succession process itself can look like a crisis, even though that's usually not the case. During succession, there may be the appearance of an underprepared successor, because the much younger successor won't have the same level of experience as her predecessor. Yet, it will work itself out . . . often with the help of willing non-family employees who step in to help fill the needs created by changing leadership.

There are times, however, when a family business finds itself on the verge or in the throes of a real crisis. We have identified five categories of real family business crises of which you should be aware.

1. THE POWER VACUUM

When there's no leadership at the top, you have a power vacuum. It may occur when a founder-CEO dies prematurely or experiences an illness that forces him to withdraw suddenly. What you may have left is a group of siblings in open conflict with one another or unprepared to work as a team, or perhaps a single unhappy heir. It's really tragic when a power vacuum results in battling adult children. All will probably try to step in and rescue the company only to discover that they lack skills, the right experience, and most important, they are not prepared to be successful as business partners. They don't have experience in working with one another as a team. They start having disagreements about the direction of the business. Suspicions arise about who's getting what. Whoever steps forward to try to help or to take responsibility for leadership becomes the target of the others. Brothers and sisters, and even cousins, don't easily accept one of their own as a leader. Conflict escalates and becomes destructive—an angry sister tells her brother, "This meeting is over and we won't have another one until you apologize!" The apology doesn't come and since they are department heads, their departments barely communicate either.

Tension continues to build, and the family and management become so focused on the conflict that the question becomes, "Who is focusing on the business?

An enlightened non-family employee can give some valuable feedback to the family. "We're really in a competitive situation," he might say, "but we're spending all our energy on this destructive, internal conflict while our competitors are using all their energy focusing on the advancement of their businesses."

A skilled, empathetic non-family employee can also tell the family what she sees and help them understand what's going on: "We don't have greedy, ignorant, selfish kids here. They're grieving and angry because they've just lost someone they love and they're taking their anger out on each other. And, they just haven't been prepared to work together effectively."

She may also help the siblings reframe the issues they are fighting about. If they are arguing over whether or not to buy an expensive computer system, perhaps she can get them to step back and think instead about what kind of decision-making mechanism is needed to lead this organization, or get them focused on "How are we going to take responsibility to run this company?"

If you are faced with battling siblings, you can even get personal: "I'm concerned about the company and, I really need you to resolve these issues." In all probability, outside help is going to be needed. You may be in a position to recommend and influence a decision to hire a professional who can be brought in to help the siblings resolve their issues and get them working together effectively as a team.

Ultimately, the family members themselves are responsible for resolving their conflicts. You can't do it for them. As in other situations, however, don't take sides. Remain neutral, be transparent, and follow protocol.

What about a power vacuum in which there is only one family member left behind to fill it? It could be a son or daughter or a spouse. We particularly like a story in which non-family employees played an extremely crucial role in helping a very young family member in a tight spot.

John Patrick (J. P.) Engelbrecht was only 22 when he was suddenly called upon to lead South Central Communications, the business founded by his grandfather. Based in Evansville, Indiana, the 325-employee company owned a television station, a string of radio stations and Muzak franchises in 10 cities. The CEO—J. P.'s father, John David Engelbrecht—had to be hospitalized for a long illness in July 2002. Suddenly, people in the company were turning to J. P. for decisions.

J. P. had broadcasting in his blood. He had worked for the business after school and in the summer since he was a boy, doing everything from cutting the grass to helping radio engineers to installing Muzak systems. Encouraged by his father, he bought his own radio station when he was 19 and leased it back to South Central. He was just out of college and had started to immerse himself in the business when his father fell ill.

Fortunately, J. P. had the support of two long-time non-family employees, CFO Bob Shirel and Jack Simmons, a division president. Both in their 50s, they had known J. P. since he was born.

"They're more than just people who work for us," J. P. told us. "They're trusted associates and friends, and they've looked after me my entire life."

Instead of brushing J. P. off because he was so young or vying for power themselves, these two men turned to him for leadership and gave him their guidance and support. They felt he had been well trained and they saw him as having maturity far beyond his years. "His big asset," said Simmons, "is looking to those around him for advice and then listening."

John David Engelbrecht returned to work on a very limited basis two months later. "You're running the company," he told his son. "Why should I take it back? Just keep running it." At a board meeting that month, J. P. was named COO and vice president.

It goes to show that even when there is no child prodigy, non-family employees can still help a young family member become a better leader. In times of crisis, the family will look to long-term key employees and professional friends for advice. Spouses who did not work in the business will want to consult those they can trust; not only about running and leading the business, but also on finance and legal matters.

2. CONTINUOUS TENSION

A business marked by continuous tension bears some similarity to the battling siblings we visited above. However, the volume is lower and the conflict is not likely to be triggered by death or illness. It just seems like it's been there and will go on forever.

When there's continuous tension, family members compete for the control of a decision. No matter what the issue is, they will take conflicting positions. Who should get a promotion? What should the dividend be? The fact that there is a legitimate issue to be resolved gets drowned out. Decisions don't get made on a timely basis or they don't get made at all, and the business suffers.

It's not that family members are competing to run the company. One might say, "I would never want the presidency." In the next breath, he'll say, "What a terrible decision my brother just made." Family members who fuel continuous tension often have well-reasoned positions, but they lack the ability to advance their views. They may look like they have ill will toward one another, but that's not necessarily so. They just can't turn a win-lose into a win-win. And some of them simply can't seem to stop complaining about everything.

Non-family employees may be tempted to write such family members off as being much more focused on beating one another than on doing what's right for the business.

Again, don't take sides. Look for creative alternatives that represent no one's position. Encourage family members to come down on the side of rationality. That allows them to resolve an issue not by saying, "I won" or "You won," but by saying, "Reason won," or "A good decision won." When a decision is crucial, it often helps to bring in an outside expert who can offer new knowledge and other perspectives on an issue when the conflict goes beyond an employee's ability to facilitate a win-win solution. An outside expert can use their objective, expert status and negotiating skills to create flexibility or to find more creative solutions that might not have emerged otherwise.

Sometimes you can be effective by seeming to do nothing. Since you know that brother Charlie complains every chance he gets and the family lets the complaining go on, just ignore him. Don't get caught up in the emotion of Charlie's complaints but focus on—and encourage the family and other employees to focus on—whether business decisions are getting made and whether they're good business decisions.

Keep reinforcing protocol. If the family in the past determined that Susan, the president, would make a certain kind of decision, remind family members that there's a mechanism in place for making the decision. Even if there's some complaining, you can support the mechanism so that the decision gets made and the business moves forward. If there is not a mechanism in place, encourage the family to develop a decision-making process, rather than getting bogged down in trying to find a solution first.

3. FUTURE DOOM

As the non-family employee, you see doom on the horizon and it's called "the kids." Maybe they're teenagers now, but you're sure they're just about the most oblivious, self-centered adolescents you've ever seen. Or they've just started working in the company and you find that they've developed a sense of entitlement, expecting more than they deserve. Because they see themselves as future owners, they take advantage of their position (arrive late, leave early), or they throw their weight around. Perhaps they are a part of a group of siblings who don't know how to get along. In hopes of peace, Mom and Dad have "siloed" them into different operations, keeping them apart. It may be false harmony, but still, in the parents' view, its harmony and for businesses needing branches or multiple semi-autonomous divisions, it works.

Your worry is that young adults like these are going to own and run the business someday. "Woe for the business," you think.

Wait a minute, though. It's really premature to be making negative judgments about the next generation. You can't really predict what teenagers are going to be like when they're mature adults, with spouses, children, and mortgages.

You may, however, be able to play a role in what shapes those future adults and even, perhaps, in how future leadership is developed and selected. If you are especially close to the owner, you can encourage a strategic planning process. A founder might not be interested in having a board of directors under "his watch," but he might be willing to have a board if he sees that it can help with succession and the choice of future leaders.

You might suggest a performance appraisal system if there's not one in place or a career development program for the younger family members coming into the business. For more information on career development programs, see *Nurturing the Talent to Nurture the Legacy: Career Development in the Family Business* by Amy M. Schuman.

You can also nudge the family to develop a portfolio of policies to guide the business, if it hasn't done so. One of the key documents would be a family employment policy that sets forth the expectations for family members who join the business. One helpful resource would be *Developing Family Business Policies: Your Guide to the Future* by Craig E. Aronoff, Ph.D., Joseph H. Astrachan, Ph.D., and John L. Ward, Ph.D. You can give a copy to the family or read it yourself and promote some of the ideas it offers.

What is important is to get started now, while next-generation family members are still young and can be guided to understand their future responsibilities and taught how to work with one another as a team.

Families often are not aware of where they are developmentally and may not know that there are preventative actions that will lead to improved functioning in the future. By bringing this to their attention, you demonstrate true concern for the business and the family that owns it. Be realistic in your expectations, however, allowing the family to consider your suggestions and adopt them at a pace they can handle.

We take heart from a story we heard about an excavation business. Everyone in the family still tells the story about an 18-year-old cousin who drove into an overpass with the crane up. That happened 20 years ago, and the cousin heard a lot about it then and still continues to hear about it. At the time of the accident, the young family member had a well-earned reputation as a daydreamer. That meant danger and doom to employees in the business that talked of his future rising through the ranks and its link to ultimate business failure. One seasoned machine operator did not join in the gossip. Instead, as the young man took on other responsibilities, the machine operator challenged the teenager's uncle who was running the business. He encouraged the uncle to make the young man's jobs explicit and put the expectations in writing. He also then encouraged that the company conduct formal performance appraisals, including progress reports from non-family employees who were critical but fair people. Now, two decades later, the "young" man is the most conscientious and dedicated of all his cousins. He grew up and matured and was helped in the process while on the job. So don't panic, but do offer solutions and join the family in seeing and appreciating their unique challenge in trying to make both family and business work in harmony.

4. FUTURE LOSSES

Losses are going to take place that will have a major impact on the family business. One might be the retirement or death (or disability) of the CEO. Another could be the death of the individual who serves as the "family glue." The family leader is a powerful person in the family, who, because he or she is so respected, manages to keep people together, holds tensions to congenial levels and mends family member relationships before they break. While this individual is alive, younger family members—siblings and cousins—behave respectfully toward one another at family social events which also spill over into the business. Often the family glue is Mom, but sometimes it's a trusted uncle or in-law. (We'll talk more about this role in the next chapter.)

The departure of either of these individuals can result in explosion. Siblings in the business erupt, or the family falls apart. Or both.

What we suggest is that the non-family employee help the family think ahead, maybe going so far as to ask the "pre-mortem" question. It is a much better alternative to a "post-mortem"—a decidedly destructive, unglamorous review of the family in the business media.[14] From a position of relative objectivity, a key employee may want to shift the attention from their conflicts with each other today, and instead ignite the family's thinking *now* about how to respond more appropriately and effectively to events that will occur later.

You may wish to address the siblings as a group: "What are you going to do when your dad's not here? Have you thought through how you're going to handle this?"

Or you can take one sibling or cousin aside: "I hear you complaining about your brother but not really doing it when your mother is in earshot. When your mother is not around, you're probably going to do it publicly. What's going to happen then?"

Or you can ask the cousins: "What are you going to do to replace the glue when Grandma dies? The business depends on the closeness of your family. Will you allow it to drift apart?"

Such questions influence family members to deal with the question, "How is it that ours will be a successful business and a successful family after mom or grandma passes away?" The idea is to get them to think beyond the possible crisis and get family members to understand that there will be a problem and they need to prepare for it now.

You may ask the questions we've suggested and not get satisfying answers. You may not be in a pivotal position to get family members to plan in this way. But it's like voting. You don't avoid voting because you think the election is going to go the other way. You still do it. There's not only an obligation, but there's a real chance that you could have significant influence here, in a direction that everyone needs from the family.

5. STAGNANT STRATEGY

The signs of a stagnant strategy are pretty clear: The business isn't growing. There has been no re-invigoration from technology. The sales department is beginning to talk about how the organization is losing once-loyal customers to other companies that can make something cheaper or provide a better service. There's no sense that the business is trying to be responsive. Efforts to get the family to consider doing things differently in order to compete more effectively seem to be met with major resistance. As a whole, people in the business have grown comfortable and have become more conservative in their thinking. Fiefdoms have developed. Energy goes into trying to maintain the status quo rather than trying to innovate and get ahead of the direction in which customers are moving.

Many family firms eventually find themselves in this situation. The business grows for years because it becomes better and better doing a few things in a well-defined market. A business that prints on other company's products is an example. Then, printing technology's increasing availability to customers and consolidation of printing businesses with aggressive expansion strategies produces competitors offering lower and lower prices. The products and services that the family firm is so proud of are being steadily reduced to commodity status.

The most critical thing you can do in this situation is to push for the introduction or reinvigoration of a strategic planning process. If top family managers aren't receptive and a direct approach won't work with them, an indirect approach might do the job. Some people argue that strategic planning is effective only if it's done from the top down. However, we have seen situations where a non-family employee starts engaging in a strategic planning process in his own department. The family CEO says, "I don't see the benefits of what you are doing," but allows the process to continue. Nine months later, that department's performance is taking off, people are excited, there's a real buzz about what's going on, and other people in the organization begin looking at that non-family employee as a leader and start calling on him for help in other areas of the company. Suddenly, you have the entire business starting to ignite from the middle rather than from the top.

The point is: Start wherever you are. Avoid criticizing the existing strategy—after all, it may be Dad's strategy and people show loyalty to him by being loyal to his strategy. Instead, initiate a planning process in your own area, asking people in your department to think about such questions as: "What parts of the existing strategy are valuable and should be kept? What changes make sense given the environment we're in and the competitive and customer markets?" Most likely, you'll look for a third option that retains important elements of the existing strategy (its underlying values and the features of the business that long-term customers most appreciate) but also adjusts to changing customer markets. Think in terms of tapping into the creativity and boldness of the founder who created the business.

The sign that you've got a good planning process in place, whether it's in a department or company-wide, is that everyone involved understands how their work connects to the over-all organization and where it's heading. People are doing their jobs not because they're told to, but because they're driving toward something.

Take care to be non-judgmental as you seek strategic change, because you're working in an area that is laden with emotion. Among the biggest obstacles may be a senior-generation member who doesn't see the need to change or junior-generation members who are trying to honor the senior generation by keeping the old strategy in place. And when one person's trying to push another to change, the first is basically saying, "What you are now doing is wrong." It can become very personal. So, while it is important to have a long-term strategic goal or vision, avoid the message that the future goal is "good" and the current strategic direction is "flawed."

What you need to do, in a sense, is to win over the heart of the controlling ownership by emphasizing the values and traits of the senior generation in a positive way and then building on that. This might mean telling the 67-year-old founder, "One of the reasons we've succeeded is that you've dominated our marketplace. We really need to get this management team to focus on what new niche markets we might penetrate and ultimately dominate."

Keep in mind, too, the possibility that the family may be open to strategic change but because everyone has been so involved in getting things done day-to-day, the issue of strategy just hasn't been raised. You may not have to prepare for war! You may only need, gently and non-judgmentally, to start getting people to think about the question, "Why are we doing what we are doing as a business?" and helping them discover what drives their decisions everyday. From there, you can ask, "Should these decision drivers be challenged?" In this way, little by little, you set the family on the road to strategic change.

Before we close this chapter, we have one more scenario we want you to consider. A man we'll call Roy is the non-family senior vice-president of Coolidge Windows, a commercial contracting company founded by Tom Coolidge 35 years ago. Roy has worked with Tom and helped the company grow for more than three decades. They've been a good team. But lately, company growth has slowed drastically, and in the last two years, Coolidge Windows has lost business with several valued customers that formerly used them exclusively. A few of the younger people in the company have been clamoring for new products to offer and urging a more aggressive approach to sales. Tom Coolidge's son and daughter, both department heads, have been defending the company's long-standing strategy of selling classic-style windows and reliable service. Roy agrees. "Coolidge built its reputation on these great old windows," he says. "Tom says he'd be ashamed to sell most of the new products we're seeing, and I think he's right."

What do you see happening here? Is it possible that the company's market has changed and that Roy has become one of the obstacles to change at Coolidge Windows?

Sometimes a bit of introspection is helpful. We find that wise non-family employees aren't afraid to ask themselves such questions as: Am I holding things back? Am I too comfortable with things the way they are? Am I keeping the business from changing?"

Chapter 10

More Understanding of the Soup You're In

That pot of soup known as family business contains more than just broth and some meat and potatoes. You'll find all kinds of vegetables and spices. In other words, it's a very complex mixture.

What we'll do in this chapter is introduce you to some of the other ingredients that go into a family business. Awareness of these ingredients should help you to further assess the business you work for. We'll throw in an idea here and there where you, the non-family employee, might take some action, but the main point of this chapter is to provide further understanding of family business.

1. MARKET AND MERIT SYSTEM VERSUS "BLOOD IS THICKER THAN WATER"

Sometimes family employees may not have the same kinds of jobs that non-family employees do. Blind or exclusive application of the market-and-merit system is simply not always appropriate in a family business. Often, a business-owning family has to find a balance between the merit system and the role and rewards of family members in the business.

Consider Luke, who has an M.B.A. and several years of outside experience under his belt. Now 36, he's joining the business and the family expects to groom him for future leadership, perhaps even the CEO role. It doesn't make sense to start Luke in an entry-level position and make him stay there for six months before he proceeds to the next level. So Luke is put into a career development process, getting a taste of each area of the company and finally being put into positions where he gets experience in supervising others.

Consider Marla, the CEO's daughter, who is the vice president of marketing. But she's also the mother of three young children and has permission to work from 10 to 4 instead of 8:30 to 5 like everyone else. It may seem unfair. Sometimes she's not available when critical decisions need to be made. But when she is on the scene, she does the work of two people and is the most successful person in that role since the company began. The family sees her as an excellent candidate to succeed the company chairman someday. Keeping her on as the marketing chief will help her understand the business thoroughly and strengthen her leadership skills.

Sometimes business families place family members in strategic slots so that they can influence everyone around them with the family's values. Other times, family members hold jobs aimed at grooming them for responsible ownership.

Instead of taking the narrow view that family members are treated with favoritism, look at the broader picture. Involving family members in more challenging roles can be a very responsible way to ensure the continuity of the business as a family enterprise; one that adheres to its values and that is properly led.

2. THE VOLUNTARY DEPARTURE OF A FAMILY MEMBER FROM THE BUSINESS

Sometimes an up-and-coming young family member, perhaps even the potential successor, leaves the business. It doesn't mean there has been a failure of some sort, nor does it have to be seen as a crisis for the business.

Family members leave for a variety of reasons. Some find that they need some distance from the family for a while in order to sufficiently distinguish themselves and make working with the family possible. Sometimes, they come back to the business. Some young family members find that when they get married, the closeness of the family makes it difficult for the newlyweds to establish themselves as an independent unit. They find the only way they can survive as a couple is to leave the business and move away. Sometimes, they come back to the business.

In other cases, the successor's dream is too different from the previous generation's dreams and he has to leave to explore his own needs and desires. We also often see an oldest son battling with Dad, only to come back six months later when the two have worked out their differences and the father is ready to pull back more. Sometimes a young family member leaves because their parents are not ready to let go and there's just not room enough for two at the top.

In still other cases, family members realize they don't want to be in business forever with their brothers and sisters or cousins. They may leave because they don't like their job. One trend we've seen is that the younger generation is much more of an advocate for a balanced lifestyle than the senior generation, who sacrificed everything for the business. The younger family member might say, "I'm traveling too much in this job and am missing seeing my children grow up." That realization may spur their departure from the family business. Finally, family members may leave when they realize they don't want to be in business forever with their brothers and sisters or cousins.

Your role? First understand that departures are normal occurrences. They happen in all businesses. Don't regard them as a crisis and don't try to reverse them—that could just prolong the problem. Don't burn your bridges with family members who leave, because they may return.

Alternatively, if given the opportunity, you can help a young person redefine their own dreams and perhaps recommit themselves to the business. You can help a daughter see that she has the strength to hang on until Dad retires in four years and at that time can recreate a business, armed with additional values, that she is uniquely capable of leading. Or you can help a son decide that he doesn't have to be the CEO; being an employee in this great business is good enough. You might help another come to the conclusion that being CEO is his life's calling—something that he's doing for himself, not for his dad or mom.

But if a family member chooses to leave, that probably is a good decision. No one should be forced to stay in the business. What you don't want to see is a 40-year-old who is unhappy in the business but who feels trapped by it because of the job opportunity and lifestyle it provides.

3. DAD AS THE GENEROUS BENEFACTOR VERSUS THE CUTTHROAT SON OR DAUGHTER

We talked earlier about how founders greatly value loyalty while their successors put more emphasis on performance and accountability. In such situations, we frequently hear long-time non-family employees describe the younger family members as "heartless" or "ruthless."

"I've worked here 25 years, giving my all, and that kid just doesn't care," a non-family employee may complain. Or, "They taught him all that M.B.A. stuff at college, and now he's trying to run this family business like a big corporation." Or, "She's just going to slice and dice the company without consideration for anything that her dad held as important."

Sometimes the younger generation is viewed as much more aggressive than the parent generation. This view of parents and offspring reflects the life-stage differences that we discussed in Chapter 5. An older parent will be more conservative, while the younger daughter and son will be much more comfortable with risk, and their aggressiveness is part of their way of putting their own mark on the business's legacy.

Yet, when younger generation family members speak of accountability and make changes that are seen as insensitive to the past sacrifices of employees, the culture is being adjusted. There may be tension between the generations while the culture shift unfolds perhaps in the form of replacing a vice president of sales that has been dad's right hand forever. Yet, it is often not as extreme a shift as it is seen to be initially. It may be the case, and often is, that some non-family employees have become less valuable in their roles as the business climate has changed. Younger family members may be eager to have the business perform to its potential and they need a strong organization that responds to their vision of the future. Sometimes they may come across as too strong and they may not always use the most diplomatic means when making changes—but recognize that change is coming and it does not mean loyalty is no longer important.

As a non-family employee, you can help keep the pendulum from swinging out to either extreme of "loyalty" or "performance" and bring it to the more balanced center of "loyalty *and* performance." In so doing, you help bridge the gap between the two generations and you demonstrate to the younger family members that you are able to adjust to the new set of rules. Recognizing and helping others to recognize that change is occurring will shorten the time span of what might otherwise have been a prolonged adjustment period characterized by resentment toward younger family members.

4. WHY FAMILY FIRMS ARE CLOSELY HELD AND SEEK TO REMAIN THAT WAY

"Why don't you take this company public?" is a question that non-family managers often ask the business owners. "Then we could raise some capital and take advantage of all these great opportunities that we've identified." Or sometimes they ask, "Why don't you provide me with the opportunity to be an owner?"

Flexibility and control are two of the reasons families keep their businesses closely held. They don't have to convince other investors to go along when they want to make changes or when they don't want to make them. While some do sell portions of their businesses in public offerings, for good reasons, most retain the ability to stay true to their values and to what they think ought to take place as opposed to what has to take place because of the pressures put on a business by outside investors. They have a strong revulsion to the regulation that might occur with Securities and Exchange Commission oversight and all the reporting that going public entails.

While it's not automatic, there is more opportunity for flexibility among family shareholders. Their demand for a return can go up and down based on the needs of the business. Minority employee shareholders will not usually be so flexible. Many families also find that the return they get by keeping their money in the business is better than what they'd realize when investing after-tax proceeds received from selling the business. This is also a reason why they don't want minority employee shareholders, who might view selling as a better investment strategy.

And, of course, as we mentioned earlier, a business is not something they own, it's something they do. It's something they love. Be cautious about pushing too hard for stock, or an IPO, as you may be tapping into a large reservoir of deeply held beliefs to stay private and family-owned forever.

5. THE ROLES THAT FAMILY MEMBERS PLAY

Different family members play different roles in a family business. You'll find these roles in almost every family business:

"Family Glue." We talked about this role in the previous chapter, when we discussed crises in family business. Sometimes this role is called "Mom" because Mom so often fills the position, especially in first-generation businesses. But we have seen many others serve as the Family Glue—a respected aunt or uncle, a grandparent, a trusted in-law, or even a sibling.

This is the person who provides the connective tissue in a family, holding the family together and guarding against the things that interfere with family relationships. Perhaps even more important, he or she inspires younger family members to manage the family glue themselves, educating them on the importance of maintaining family relationships. "Call your brother," she may say. "He's having a tough time." Or she may help two battling siblings find a way to maintain their relationship despite the challenges they pose to each other.

The person who fills this role may not be in the business and you may wonder if there is such a person and if one is really needed. But make no mistake. This is a very powerful role and one that is critical to the success of the business. He or she provides the leadership that helps unite the family so that its members can come together and support the family business.

When the CEO's wife appears at the office or asks a question, the wise non-family employee does not write her off as an interfering woman. Instead, he recognizes that she might be acting as the Family Glue. If that seems to be the case, he supports her involvement instead of politely ignoring or rebuffing her, with the wise understanding that she plays a valuable role in enhancing the business's stability and making it possible for the next generation to work together as a team.

In-laws. Unfortunately, family members and non-family employees often view the in-laws as trouble. They're seen as people who should be guarded against. The irony is, if the in-laws feel that they are being totally excluded from any influence on the organization that so influences their own families, they can become hostile. This doesn't mean they have to be included in decision making.

But, if they are included in information sharing and their opinions and support are sought as values are instilled in the business or the next generation, they can be a great asset.

Being an in-law is a tough job. In-laws don't have a good set of rules that tell them where they fit in. They have to find their own place in the family. If they work in the business, they want to succeed. They want to be recognized for their own achievements, which may be difficult to do when they're labeled as family employees and seen as people who perhaps haven't earned their keep.

As a non-family employee, you can drop whatever stereotypes you might have about in-laws and recognize the difficult position they're in. Assume that the more knowledgeable about the business and culture in-laws are, the more positive an influence they will be. And if you have the opportunity, you can facilitate their understanding of the family business and help them be an asset, not an enemy. But don't try to use them as a pipeline to the CEO when you're upset about something. Although they may hold a position of responsibility, they might not be in a position to be helpful and that would cause awkwardness. Go direct to the CEO instead.

Inactive Family Shareholders. The more family shareholders a business has, the more likely there will be some who are resentful and dissatisfied. And sometimes, they have reasons to be demanding and angry that are not so apparent to others. They may be children of a founder who worked 80 hours a week and was virtually absent to them as a parent. Or their second-generation father worked under a founder who belittled him and made him miserable.

While family members inside the business may think these shareholders should be totally grateful for what they have, the shareholders themselves don't feel like what they are receiving is an inheritance or gift at all. To them, their shares and any dividends they receive are an earned payout for a form of sweat equity that they gave as children and young adults. They may have sacrificed a lot in childhood, and now they have strong feelings about having some kind of voice in the business even though they don't work for it. Their attitude is, "I've had to put up with this for 50 years, and I've earned this dividend!"

Family members working in the company sometimes treat the inactive shareholders as enemies who want the business's capital and desire things for themselves that they don't deserve. The insiders believe that greater involvement of inactive shareholders will only harm the business. They may have experienced criticism from their inactive cousins who justify their views of company management with, "Grandfather would never approve of what you are doing with the company he founded." Faced with what they see as inappropriate and undermining, a besieged branch involved in managing the business may even present inactive shareholders with a proposal to sell their shares so that they don't have to be accountable to them.

In the best business-owning families we have known, shares are viewed as a stewardship responsibility to be held and passed down to the next generation like a family heirloom.

It's helpful to understand that inactive shareholders will differ in their emotions and expectations. Some will treat their shares as a pure investment, while others will view their ownership as a well-deserved inheritance, and others may view their shares as "special," making them a part of the business and sometimes much too active in management decision making. Finally, in the best business-owning families we have known, shares are viewed as a stewardship responsibility to be held and passed down to the next generation like a family heirloom.

Try not to get caught up in the family members' different views of one another. If the opportunity presents itself, you can encourage the family to answer such questions as: What is the role of inactive family shareholders? What might be the value of inactive family members to the business? How can we appropriately involve inactive shareholders and be one shareholder team rather than two or three?

These are issues that the family must resolve for itself, but you might be in a position to put the questions out there.

The Founder. Founders have been discussed at length in Chapter 5, so let us here just remind you how complex and contradictory they can be. They want what's best for the business even though they might not be acting like they do in certain situations. They certainly want what's best for the family, although they may seem to ignore how their unilateral business decisions impact the family. They created the business from nothing and they're often convinced it can't succeed without them, so they have difficulty letting go of control. All this is predictable and normal and part of the reality of a family business.

6. FAMILY MEETINGS—A BOON OR BOONDOGGLE?

You observe that all the family owners, their spouses, and their children head for the shareholders meeting one year in Vail, the next year in Banff, and the year after that in Puerto Rico. Or they have a "family retreat" in Hawaii.

All boondoggles? No. Family meetings play an invaluable role in strengthening a family firm and contributing to its stability. Such gatherings reinforce the family glue by enabling family members to have fun together. At the same time, the family is using these assemblies as opportunities to educate family members about the business, establish common expectations and work toward a unified voice. Family members also engage in joint planning and communicate with one another about such things as buy-sell agreements and estate planning.

Younger family members need to be prepared for their future roles as family shareholders and business partners. Young in-laws with small children may not see the value in arranging childcare and attending educational seminars or family meetings. Strong families have found that the incentive value of an appealing location encourages attendance, provides an opportunity to strengthen the glue that must bind a growing family, and creates a forum for their joint work of preparing for the future.

7. SIBLINGS AND COUSINS

Let's go back to our soup metaphor. Siblings and cousins are very different ingredients, and it's important to understand that. The sibling relationship is very intense. Having a common set of parents allows siblings to develop certain expectations of each other based on their upbringing. Because of their need to feel equally loved by their parents, siblings often favor equal compensation and seek to be equally valued for their skills, even though they may not produce equal results for the business. Sibling rivalry develops as sons and daughters compete for all the things of value that parents can grant to young family members.

Some sibling groups are highly skilled at working together in a collaborative fashion. Many others are not. It's very common for siblings to seek individual and distinct areas in which to shine and be recognized. Yet, when they don't receive the recognition they seek, they may become "siloed" in the organization, with each overseeing their own fiefdom. As we have noted earlier, parents may intentionally silo the siblings if they feel that the children cannot work together effectively. Or they make two brothers copresidents because they cannot choose, sometimes with good business results and at other times with not.

Siblings in some families don't talk to each other very much; they just do their jobs. It's a mistake, however, to assume that they are totally disconnected from one another. They actually love each other and harbor common values or a common vision for they business.

The intensity of the sibling generation generally doesn't carry over to the cousins in a family business, and cousins tend to be less concerned about being treated equally with one another. There may be a greater disparity of beliefs among the cousins, due in large part to not growing up in the same home and the influence that the cousins' spouses have brought into the family or the fact that some of the cousins live far away. Rivalries and differences among the siblings may influence the cousins to view other family branches has having some deficiencies.

Often, the problem in the founding and sibling generations is that family members are too enmeshed in the business and can't separate themselves from it. In the cousin generation, however, the problem becomes one of needing to draw the cousins closer together and closer to the business to help them feel connected to it.

8. FAMILY CULTURE

Whether it is a sibling generation or a cousin generation, the business is the underlying cultural uniqueness of the owning family. Examining the family's culture can provide you with good information that will help you work well with the business and the family. Take a look at the family and think about the rules that you see guiding it. Is the family more open or more closed? That is, do family members express ideas openly or not? Do they share information freely? Are conflicts aired or suppressed? Do family members talk about finances or are finances taboo?

Look at other ways the family might be unique. Some families parent more rigidly, while others parent more loosely. Some families take vacations together; others vacation separately.

Ethnic heritage will also play a part in the family's culture, influencing its communication style (expressive or quiet and repressed, for example) or its apparent ways of managing how decisions are made. Does Dad seem to make them all, or does the family seek input from everyone and try for consensus? How conflict is managed is another key indicator of family culture. Some families confront each other easily and get issues resolved quickly. Others appear to live by the motto "peace at any price." These families prefer to let conflicts remain under the surface, unaddressed, resisting all suggestions to air their grievances with each other.

You can use Exhibit 5, "Assumed Rules Operating in Families," as a tool to help you further analyze the culture of the family you work for. We have used it with family members to help them identify the unspoken as well as the spoken rules that guide the family. We also ask them to think about how the changing needs of the family make these rules either strengths or obstacles to family success. You might do the same, thinking instead of the changing needs of the family business.

EXHIBIT 5   **Assumed Rules Operating in Families**

Directions
First, identify the specific family group (nuclear, extended, etc.) that you wish to consider. Then, for each of the rules listed below, identify the point on the continuum where you believe the family group you are considering best fits currently.

Category	Mid-point	
Information Sharing	Open............	............Closed
Decision Making	Collaborative............	............Autocratic
Social Presentation	Casual............	............Formal
Consumption	Thrifty............	............Conspicuous
Extended Family Togetherness	Frequent............	............Infrequent
Conflict	Open............	............Closed
Unearned Resources	Stewardship............	............Entitlement
Recreation	Together............	............Independent
In-laws & the Business	Involved............	............Not Involved
Household Order	Exact............	............Chaotic
Traditions	Deeply Rooted............	............Not Celebrated

Understanding these additional cultural factors that define a family business can provide non-family employees with a bigger picture and restrain them from making premature or mistaken judgments about a family. We find that the most successful non-family employees are those who search for a deeper knowledge of the family and its history as well as the motivations and special circumstances of the members within it. They do this in order to understand and accurately predict what will or will not work in the family business in which they are a member.

Chapter 11

The Empowered Employee

Maximizing Your Success

You can be a good non-family employee, or you can be a great one—an employee of exceptional, indispensable value to a family firm. What makes the difference? You've already been exposed to a wide range of ideas about the contributions that you can make to a family firm and have been offered suggestions for career-harming traps to avoid. What we want to do here is to enlarge your view of what it means to be an employee in a family firm and to show you how you can turn that role into something very special by becoming an *empowered* non-family employee. In essence, with knowledge, imagination, and sensitivity, you might transform the work that you do from a job to an engaging and more fulfilling career.

To begin, let's review some of the major principles that have been introduced in other contexts throughout this book:

◆ Empowered non-family employees take the time to get to know the business-owning family they work for and to seek to understand what the family is going through and what kind of an environment it is that pulls the members in so many directions. They do not prejudge family members or write the family off as incompetent.

◆ As they gain understanding of family business dynamics, empowered non-family employees develop empathy for the family and devote themselves to being members of the family's team, rather than viewing the family as the enemy and fighting it.

◆ Empowered family managers take the initiative. Instead of playing victim to what some might see as the family's ineptness ("The family will never buy this great idea of mine!") or waiting for conflicted family members to get their act together, empowered employees advance solutions and do so in appropriate ways. They realize the mistake in underpreparing younger family members for future leadership. Instead of watching the game, they're in the game.

◆ Empowered employees follow the medical maxim of "First, do no harm." They don't involve themselves in family issues unless they can be helpful. They avoid such traps as taking sides or getting trapped as the third part of a triangle. They know their strengths and limitations.

◆ Empowered employees understand the family's values and play by the family's rules, whether spoken or unspoken. They also follow protocol, being straightforward and transparent in their actions. They know that making end runs bypassing a family member while involving another higher up can destroy hard-won trust.

◆ Empowered employees have the courage to contribute their ideas and honest opinions. They know it's not helpful to retreat to the position, "It's your business and you can do what you want with it." They also know if they have enough political capital to say something important to a family CEO she may not want to hear. They are respectful and tactful in giving their opinions. As Jack Simmons, the non-family division president at South Central Communications puts it: "I let them know right up front that it's their organization, and my job is to administrate their wishes, but here's what I think."

◆ Empowered employees see the bigger picture. They understand that a supportive family is an asset to the business and not something to be set apart from the enterprise. They help the business to serve as an expression of family values, and they encourage trust among family members, both those inside the business as well as inactive family shareholders.

Beyond these important characteristics and roles of empowered employees are three other major topics that bear discussion: "political capital," mentoring, and fostering effective family involvement.

UNDERSTANDING "POLITICAL CAPITAL"

Your ability to make a positive contribution to sensitive situations in a family firm is related to how much "political capital"[15] you have. Political capital involves the family members' respect for you and your knowledge and opinions, and the trust they place in you. You have high political capital when your relationship with the family is very close and trusting. You'll know, because you will have been brought in for heart-to-heart discussions with family members in the past and they will seek your advice on sensitive issues. A parent may say to you, "I just don't know what I'm going to do about my son." Or a sister may tell you, "If my brother and I keep fighting, one of us is going to have to leave." They express heartfelt statements instead of lashing out angrily about a relative.

The more political capital you have, the more risk you can take in venturing opinions, advancing solutions, or stepping in to help mitigate family conflicts. When your political capital is high, you have more options available to you. You can address personal issues or suggest an idea that might be adverse to the family's views, but they'll cut you some slack. They'll trust your motivation and not be suspicious of the intrusion into something that is normally private.

If your political capital is low, however, you don't dare make such intrusions. Your options are much more limited.

It's important to assess yourself accurately in terms of how much political capital you have. Non-family employees who overrate their political capital and overstep boundaries with the family run the risk of serious damage to their careers.

You can develop and build your political capital, but it takes patience, time, and a history of demonstrating diplomacy and trustworthiness and excellent job performance.

Consider the Mechanics Bank non-family CEO Bill Reid, whom you met in Chapter 2. Reid found himself in a very sensitive situation several years ago, a situation that called not only on his knowledge and skills but also on the sizable political capital he had developed. The Mechanics Bank is a majority-owned, 100-year-old regional bank in Northern California. It is owned by a family in its third and fourth generation. Overcoming their limited trust of one another, the branches of the family agreed to add new members to their board. All the branches were concerned about who the directors might be and whether they would be biased toward one branch or another.

It was at this point that Bill Reid went to each of the branches and exercised his considerable political capital. Bill surprised everyone saying, "I have three candidates that fit your qualifications that I recommend highly." The leaders of all the family branches immediately recognized exceptional qualifications and the candidates sailed through the nominating process and were elected quickly.

What Reid demonstrated was an exceptional ability to navigate between family branches and he had earned the political capital to do so. The family was rewarded for its trust in his judgment—greater effectiveness of their board allowed the family to make tremendous progress toward family unity and trust.

ARE YOU A POTENTIAL MENTOR?

Oftentimes, non-family executives, managers, and trusted employees are called upon to be mentors to younger family members, and this is a valuable and legitimate service to perform. However, not everyone is well-prepared or cut out for this role. Some people just don't have the patience or temperament for it. Others, however, enjoy helping younger people learn and develop. You will want to be honest with yourself and the family about whether you have the desire and ability to be a mentor.

In our view, some qualifications need to be met. Ideally, the mentor is ten or more years older than the person being mentored. A mentor also needs to be accomplished in the skills that the younger person needs to develop. If a young family member is taking on a new-product development task, he or she can gain a great deal of knowledge from a mentor who has taken an idea from the concept stage and brought it to market.

Jack Pycik, an executive we know, says, "Everyone has to understand that my obligation is totally to the one I am mentoring." He suggests these attributes of a good mentor:

- Above-average, nonjudgmental listening skills.

- Respect for confidentiality. A good rule to follow is: "Anything I say can be repeated to anyone the family member wants to tell, and nothing that the family member says to me will be repeated to anyone without his or her expressed approval."

- Integrity. The mentor should be honest with the family member and information gleaned from a discussion should never be used against the family member in anger or to gain an advantage of some kind.

- Experience in business, family, and society.

- A history of success in multiple environments.

An attribute we would add is the ability to avoid acting out one's will through the young family member. This person needs to be able to follow their own path. If a mentor really needs the young family member to do what he's told, that's a supervisor-subordinate relationship, not a mentor-protégé relationship.

Mentors also need to be secure in their role. If the protégé complains about Dad's lack of information-sharing, the mentor avoids agreeing and promising to argue the young person's case with Dad. Instead, she asks, "How are you going to make that point clearly to your father in a way that he can accept?" If you think you're susceptible to being seduced into a fight with Dad, you can either disqualify yourself from being a mentor to begin with, or you can put yourself on the alert against being co-opted.

What if you find yourself in a potentially difficult situation as a mentor? You're caught in the middle because Dad is demanding that you reveal what his son is saying in the mentoring sessions, for example, or insisting on a particular outcome from the process. In such circumstances, it's better to encourage the family to engage someone such as an independent individual outside the business with the right background and chemistry as a mentor or coach, who doesn't face the same loyalty issues.

Remember that mentoring is not a life-long commitment. It could be as short as six months. The executive we mentioned above says that he leaves it up to the person he's mentoring to decide whether or not to continue the process. At the end of every session, this mentor asks, "Would you like to schedule another meeting?" And, he adds, "I always leave the protégé an opportunity for a gracious exit."

SUPPORTING EFFECTIVE FAMILY INVOLVEMENT

Most business-owning families want effective, appropriate representation in the business and they are very likely looking to you, the non-family employee, to support them in accomplishing that goal. They want some special consideration for their ownership and the value that they bring to the business as a family. And while it may not seem like it sometimes, they don't want you to be passive. Yes, they want your support, yet they want you to diplomatically resist when you feel their involvement is inappropriate. They may need your help in defining what is an appropriate role for the family at large, as well as a family's role in certain situations.

What is appropriate involvement of family in the business? It may be helpful first to point out what it is not: a family who says, "This company is an employment agency for our family, so any family member gets a job here." Or, "I can do anything I want because I'm an owner."

Appropriate involvement means that family members meet qualifications if they wish to be employed by the business. There is consideration of the needs of the business, the needs of the job, and how the capabilities of an individual meet the needs of the job. When both family and non-family candidates meet the qualifications, a family still might legitimately come down on the side of the family applicant because of the values and vision that the family brings to the business. The family applicant may also provide the family continuity in the business that is important to its long-term success.

The concept of appropriate involvement also applies to family shareholders who do not work in the business. A group of knowledgeable, supportive shareholders can be one of a family firm's most treasured assets. The role you can play as a non-family employee is to encourage family managers to be active in keeping shareholders informed, providing opportunities for valuable influence and fostering their education as responsible owners. You will find useful background and insights in *Family Business Ownership: How to Be an Effective Shareholder* by Craig E. Aronoff, Ph.D., and John L. Ward, Ph.D.

One family took their involvement as outside shareholders seriously and, as they were often subject to being drawn into company employee relations issues, they decided to create for themselves a code of conduct. Working with senior non-family management, they developed the following rules:

1. We will speak well of each other to anyone outside the family. This will be especially the case when we are, from time

to time, confronted or engaged by employees. We will keep all family business discussions private.

2. We will always respect the opinion of others. We commit to resolve our disagreements constructively and not to interfere in the need for business employees to constructively resolve their own conflicts.

3. When confronted by an employee or customer about an injustice, we will encourage them to contact the appropriate person in the company. However, it is understood that we might directly ask a question of one of the vice presidents, as this is appropriate and encouraged by senior management. The issue may be resolved by this action or diminish as a problem by getting more information. That is, it is important to try to learn as much as possible as sometimes an issue is better understood by learning from management, who are committed to helping shareholders understand company policy.

4. We expect family members to be themselves when interacting with employees. We will conduct ourselves in a way that will not be detrimental to the image of the company and that will not be in any way different than what we expect of our employees.

5. When family members attend company functions, we will adhere to the same employment policies we have for non-family employees of the company.

When non-family employees resist any involvement by the family shareholders, employees can lose their value to the firm, even when their job performance appears excellent. There is a non-family CEO we know of who leads a third-generation family firm in Canada. He has a good board of directors, dominated by non-family independent directors who each bring different strategic perspectives from their backgrounds and capabilities. The board functions well and is very supportive of the CEO. But the CEO only communicates to shareholders at the annual shareholder meeting, as directed by law. Our prediction is that this particular CEO may be terminated in three-to-five years. We have seen the situation too many times. Up until his departure, his performance will be good, and the company will do well. However, in his view of the proper separation of family and business, his behavior will create the effect of making people feel excluded from their business. Instead of accommodating and demonstrating openness to the family group about what constitutes appropriate family involvement, he resists in a hundred different ways. His model for the business is a public company where shareholders' only interaction with the company occurs through the board of directors or at the annual shareholders meeting.

We've all had the experience of dealing with a retail service person who weighs our request against a faceless company policy. He can prove he is adhering to all of the requirements of his job. And we have all experienced an entirely different service person—one who is truly interested in and cares about our needs. The CEO described previously is like the former; he accomplishes policy yet alienates himself from the family. His actions say, "This is not a family business, and you are just one of several shareholders. I run the business." Eventually, the family will put pressure on the board for a change. With sensitivity to the demands of running a business, which is hard enough by itself, there is another job for senior non-family employees. Supporting and helping to manage the interaction between the business and inactive family shareholders.

By exercising every opportunity to see the larger picture and to perform as an empowered employee, you make yourself more and more indispensable to the family and its business. You provide more value, and you are more valued in return. An entirely different position of a non-family CEO is demonstrated in a letter written to the founder of a business that was transitioning from an entrepreneurial company to a family business (see Exhibit 6). The CEO, initially reluctant and concerned about "family intrusions," learned over five years how to adopt a supportive stance.

EXHIBIT 6   Letter to the Family

1/29/04
Dear Joe and family,

As the fifth year of my tenure as CEO draws to an end and the company celebrates its 40th anniversary, I thought this would be a perfect time to reflect on what I have come to realize about the extraordinary nature of working in a family company. When I first arrived at the Jones Corporation, I knew this was a place in which I could flourish. Jones Corp. had everything that was important to me at the time, a great product with a niche market, a strong balance sheet, and an excellent work environment. I could capitalize on these foundation elements and make the owners wealthy. However, after five years, I've come to realize how short-sighted I was. Working for Joe Sr. has given me a chance to learn about true leadership, not of a business, but of a family business.

I must admit, when young, inexperienced and, as he now says so himself, somewhat overconfident, Joe Jr. came into the business followed closely by his younger sister and brother, I thought I was seeing the beginning of the end. It seemed as though providing jobs to three untrained, inexperienced young family members would distract us from what the business could become. The immediate, intruding family conflicts that followed their arrival reinforced my concerns. I became convinced they were an immense liability and I anticipated difficult times ahead. Then Joe Sr. started the family meetings with all of the outside shareholders with the predictable outcome, it seemed to me, to provide a forum for several family shareholders who have never worked for Jones Corp. to get involved in management of the company. If I had my concerns before, I knew we were now on a path that would divert us from the true potential of the company and render us mediocre.

Not long afterward, when Joe Sr. and Joe Jr. began to have confrontations over the direction of the company, there were many nights I told my wife how difficult it was to be in a situation where the family issues seemed to be overtaking our attention to this wonderful business opportunity. As you now know, my goal at the time was to keep my head down and stay out of what I perceived to be family squabbles. In fact, there were many times I wished your conflicts had been kept totally separate from the management team and me.

Now, five years later, I see this family business in a totally different light. I realize that the tension between Joe Sr. and Joe Jr. wasn't just a family conflict, but was a struggle to forge the very best strategy that our company could pursue for the long-term health of the organization, integrating the family and shareholder group. I realize that the conflicts during management meetings weren't family discussions that needed to be separate from the business, but were discussions that needed to play out between two important managers in the business whose family identities are as much a part of the Jones Corp. fabric as is our niche market, balance sheet, and work environment. In fact, because of the conflict that you so openly had in our strategic planning sessions and your willingness to invite management into the dialogue, I believe we have a future company that is a much stronger company than the one I had envisioned for you when I joined; one that will be strong for another generation with involved family shareholders who are part of the solution.

While I initially viewed your children as a liability, I've now come to appreciate their fierce loyalty to the success of the organization and have enjoyed watching all three in different circumstances serve as ambassadors to the organization, using the family name as a competitive advantage, winning contracts with customers and negotiating with vendors. I have also shifted from thinking of the outside family shareholder group as a potential hindrance to continuity and I now see them as the key to continuity of the business.

Joe, there was a time when I wished you would provide protection from your family for all of us non-family employees. I now realize it wasn't protection we needed, it was inclusion in the family, just as you included your family in the business. I think you have provided an excellent example of the kind of inclusion we needed; you mixed us together to create long-term business solutions and did not protect either from the other. As a consequence, when I first came, I joined a company, and now I have joined a family company.

I wish the entire family continued success and I look forward to the many ways we will work as a team.

Regards,
Stephen Mason Reges
CEO

Chapter 12

Summary

Do you now have a different perspective on what it means to be an effective non-family employee? We certainly hope so. When you accept that "the family is part of the territory" instead of trying to isolate the family from the business, your job takes on much greater depth and breadth. The work you do will likely be richer and your value to the business and its successful future will be greater. You will distinguish yourself as someone who is on the family business team.

As a reader of this book, you have demonstrated that you have already absorbed one of the most important points we want to make: that it's necessary to take time to understand the family business. You have shown that you are willing to be nonjudgmental and keep an open mind about what you see. You've discovered that family conflict, sibling rivalry, nepotism, and other so-called family business characteristics are not necessarily threatening. You now know that it's shortsighted to jump to the conclusion that these are "bad" or the result of a dysfunctional family. You've learned that they are a normal part of family business and that every business-owning family has issues it must resolve. What's more, you've learned that you can play a valuable role in helping the family, as long as you have the knowledge and skills to do so when it's appropriate—as well as the wisdom to stand back and do nothing when doing something would do more harm than good.

You've also learned more about the family business "system" and how three components—family, management, and ownership—overlap one another and how it's sometimes difficult for family members to sort out which role they're playing at any given time. Family member? Manager? Owner?

By now, you have also probably gained a new understanding of how, in most cases, the presence of family benefits a business. Perhaps you've been doing some thinking about the specific business you work for and how the owning family is of value to it—or how it could be, if you encouraged the family to become more involved in appropriate and effective ways. We hope you have warmed to the idea that the integration of family into the business is an enlightened one. The family just needs to find the right level of integration, and you can play a valuable role in helping it to do so.

You have also discovered some ways of staying out of trouble. Don't side with one family member against another, or with one generation over another. Play by the family's cultural rules. Follow protocol and keep your actions transparent. It's not possible to cover all the difficult situations you might find yourself in, but we hope we've given you the insights and tools you need to come up with your own solutions when a new problem confronts you.

You should have also gained some ideas for assessing yourself. Perhaps you've decided you need more political capital and have begun to outline some ways to build it. Or perhaps you now realize what a good mentor you could be. Or maybe you have begun to make a list of skills you'd like to develop so that you can effectively help family members reframe their conflicts, learn to negotiate better, or be a better listener when they share their concerns.

There are many pathways to being a more valuable non-family employee, but all of them lead to seeing yourself as a member of the family's team and helping it get where it wants to go. As a non-family employee, you have a unique opportunity. What a wonderful challenge it will be to make the most of it.

Notes

1. Binzen, Peter. "A Small Specialty Brew with Strong Brand Loyalty." *Philadelphia Inquirer*, Nov. 24, 2003: pp. D1, D7.
2. Pompilio, Natalie. "Melrose Diner Honored as a Great Place to Work." *Philadelphia Inquirer*, Nov. 27, 2003: A1, A15.
3. Ibid.
4. International Family Enterprise Research Academy. "Family Businesses Dominate." *Family Business Review*, vol. 16, no. 4 (December 2003): pp. 235–239.
5. Astrachan, Joseph H., and Melissa Carey Shanker. "Family Businesses' Contribution to the U.S. Economy: A Closer Look." *Family Business Review*, vol. 16, no. 3 (September 2003): pp. 211–219.
6. Ibid.
7. *American Family Business Survey*. 2003. MassMutual Financial Group and the George and Robin Raymond Family Business Institute.
8. Holcomb, Henry J. "Family History Lends Value to Binswanger Firm." *Philadelphia Inquirer*, Nov. 17, 2003, pp. D1, D11.
9. "Consumers Trust Family Business Products." *The Family Business Advisor*, vol. XI, no. 2 (February 2002): p. 1.
10. Pompilio, op. cit.
11. *American Family Business Survey*, op. cit.
12. Simurda, Stephen J. "Eric Monsen's Mentoring Team." *Family Business* (Winter 1995): pp. 24–29.
13. "Family Employment Guidelines." The Widmer Stewardship, Widmer Interiors, Peoria, IL.
14. Aronoff, Craig E. "Pre-Mortem Beats Post-Mortem." *Family Business Advisor*, vol. XI, no. 4 (April 2002): p. 1.
15. Our mentor, colleague, and partner, John L. Ward, introduced us to this term in another context. Yet it fits perfectly with the point we are making.

Suggested Additional Readings

Aronoff, Craig E., and John L. Ward. *Family Business Governance: Maximizing Family and Business Potential*, Marietta, GA: Family Business Consulting Group/New York: Palgrave Macmillan, 2011.

Aronoff, Craig E., and John L. Ward. *Preparing Your Family Business for Strategic Change*, Marietta, GA: Family Business Consulting Group/New York: Palgrave Macmillan, 2011.

Aronoff, Craig E., Joseph H. Astrachan, and John L. Ward. *Developing Family Business Policies: Your Guide to the Future*, Marietta, GA: Family Business Consulting Group/New York: Palgrave Macmillan, 2011.

Astrachan, Joseph H., and Kristi S. McMillan. *Conflict and Communication in the Family Business*, Marietta, GA: Family Enterprise Publishers, 2003.

Carlock, Randel S., and John L. Ward. *Strategic Planning for the Family Business: Parallel Planning to Unify the Family and Business*, New York: Palgrave, 2001.

Gersick, Kelin E., John A. Davis, Marion McCollom Hampton, and Ivan Lansberg. *Generation to Generation: Life Cycles of the Family Business*, Boston: Harvard Business School Press, 1997.

Goleman, Daniel. *Emotional Intelligence: Why It Can Matter More Than IQ*, New York: Bantam Books, 1995.

———. *Working with Emotional Intelligence*, New York: Bantam Books, 1998.

Lansberg, Ivan. *Succeeding Generations: Realizing the Dream of Families in Business*, Boston: Harvard Business School Press, 1999.

O'Hara, William T. *Centuries of Success: Lessons from the World's Most Enduring Family Businesses*, Avon, MA: Adams Media, 2004.

Schuman, Amy M. *Nurturing the Talent to Nurture the Legacy: Career Development in the Family Business*, Marietta, GA: Family Business Consulting Group/ New York: Palgrave Macmillan, 2011.

Tifft, Susan E., and Alex S. Jones. *The Trust: The Private and Powerful Family Behind The New York Times*, Boston: Little Brown and Co. 1999.

Ward, John L. *Perpetuating the Family Business: 50 Lessons from Long-Lasting, Successful Families in Business*, New York: Palgrave, 2004.

Index

The Authors

Chris Eckrich, Ph.D., is a Principal Consultant of the Family Business Consulting Group, Inc., and specializes in building leadership excellence and maintaining family unity in family-owned businesses. He is also an Adjunct Professor at the University of Notre Dame.

Stephen L. McClure is a Principal Consultant at the Family Business Consulting Group, Inc., and specializes in family communications and decision making, succession planning and implementation, and governance and management in family firms.

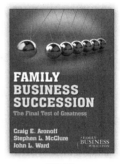

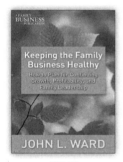
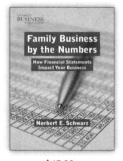